76 Ways

TO USE

NONI FRUIT J

For Your Better He

PRIDE

PUBLISHING

PRAISE FOR:
76 WAYS TO USE NONI FRUIT JUICE

"Isa Navarre has done a masterful job. [This Book] is certain to help the newcomer as well as the long-time user of Noni fruit juice in showing the myriad uses for this amazing product."

– Donald J. Mantell, M.D.

"This book answered many of the questions that people are continually asking us about how to use the Noni fruit juice for various applications. We found it very insightful and quite informative. We feel that anyone who uses the Noni would benefit from a thorough reading of *76 Ways to Use Noni Fruit Juice*. It is now kept in our medical reference library to be used as the need arises. We would suggest that any believer in the healing properties of the Noni plant do the same."

– Floyd and Ann Holdman

"When I first started taking Noni, it cleared my arthritis. But after a while, the pain returned. Then I tried one of the techniques in this book—Interrupting Noni Therapy—and it worked! Noni is now helping my arthritis better than before. Besides being an arsenal of tools for using Noni, *76 Ways to Use Noni* is an excellent marketing tool, and I would recommend that everyone have a copy."

– Sal Serio

"*76 Ways to Use Noni* is a fascinating book. It provides simple, easy-to-use techniques for using Noni in almost every situation. The remedy for tooth aches and the Headache Compress have done wonders for my family, and my 4 year old son, Josh, who is a diabetic takes Noni regularly. Not only did we try the ideas for giving Noni to children, but we also tell Josh he will get muscles like the man on the front of the bottle and that has done wonders! He calls Noni his "muscle juice" and compares himself to the man with every dose. I also noticed amazing results when I gave Josh the Noni before every meal rather than just a morning dose. The suggestions in this book for using Noni fruit juice for diabetes really have made a difference!

"This book is exactly what the world needs, with helpful remedies in an easy to read format. Now Noni users everywhere can experience the miraculous benefits from Noni in more ways than just taking a daily dose. Isa has done an incredible job introducing Noni and its benefits to the world."

–Emily Freeman

By the same author:

42 WAYS TO USE NONI SKIN LOTION

A Handbook of Topical Applications

HEALING SECRETS OF NONI

A Practical Guide to Noni Dilutions and Harmonics

76 Ways

TO USE
NONI FRUIT JUICE
For Your Better Health

A HANDBOOK OF ORAL, TOPICAL
AND INTERNAL APPLICATIONS AND PROCEDURES

ISA NAVARRE

Pride Publishing
500 South Geneva Road
Vineyard, Utah 84058

76 Ways to Use Noni Fruit Juice for Your Better Health
A Handbook of Oral, Topical and Internal
Applications & Procedures

Copyright © 2001 Isa Navarre

Illustrated by Valerie Mortensen.
Cover Design by Robert Evelyn Design Group.
Back Cover Photo by Robert Norman Photography.
Printed in the United States of America.
ISBN 1-887938-99-0

– IMPORTANT NOTICE –

The information in this book is designed to provide health information for purposes of reference and guidance and to accompany, not replace, the services of a qualified health care practitioner or physician. It is not the intent of the author or publisher to prescribe any substance to cure, mitigate, treat, or prevent any disease. In the event you use this information with or without seeking medical attention, the author and publisher shall not be liable or otherwise responsible for any loss, damage or injury caused or arising out of, directly or indirectly, by the information contained in this book or its use.

DEDICATION

My daughter, Aria Ray, was born two weeks after I started taking Noni fruit juice. The idea for this book came soon afterwards. I felt it was significant that her birth, my introduction to Noni, and the idea for this book happened so closely together.

In ancient Polynesia, knowledge of healing was conveyed from one generation to the next. This book is helping me follow that tradition. Moreover, it will help introduce Noni to families all over the world. I feel very blessed to be part of that. And so, I dedicate this book to children everywhere, and in particular, to Aria Ray and Kellan, my daughters who were born since I began taking Noni.

CONTENTS

SECTION 2:
TOPICAL APPLICATIONS 141

ACKNOWLEDGEMENTS

In thinking about the many who supported and contributed to this book, my gratitude must go first to Nature herself, for developing the remarkable *Morinda citrifolia*, or Noni plant, and then to generations of Polynesians whose use of the Noni fruit left the world a powerful legacy.

May I also take this opportunity to personally thank Mitchell Tate for "finding" Noni and bringing it to the attention of John Wadsworth and Stephen Story, world-renowned food scientists, who made Noni palatable for modern tastebuds. Thank you also to Kerry Asay, Kim Asay, and Kelly Olsen for their untiring effort to help bring Noni fruit juice to the world, and to the President of French Polynesia, Mssr. Gaston Floss, and the Country's Vice-President, Mssr. Edouard Fritch, for their generous support of Noni agriculture and export. Many thanks are also due Dr. Annie Hirazumi, Dr. Ralph Heinicke, Dr. Charles Garnier, and researchers of Noni around the world for their efforts and inspiration to examine Noni scientifically.

The original version of this book, titled *"53 Ways to Use Noni,"* was first published in 1998. I would like to continue to recognize those who helped me with that book because my gratitude to you is sincerely heartfelt. I wish to thank all of you, and in particular, Catherine Sarnoski, Dennis and Carol Kotopoulis, Don and Nancy Failla, Carol LaBarge, Tina Erwin, Glenn Raney, Jay Coons, Dave Peacock, Kent Murphy, Bonnie and Bob Landino, Helen King, Ann Eckroth, Jodie Snyder, and Becky Yoder for her help with the Noni Colonic Irrigation, Dr. Don Mantell for his marvelous enthusiasm, and Dr. Ken Stejskal for his open-hearted anticipation of the book.

Special thanks also to friends who agreed to review the manuscript and/or offer their feedback or endorsement: Floyd and Ann, Tom and Mannie, Ken and Mary, Sal and Joan, Del and Sylvia, and Dr. Bryant Bloss.

I am also very grateful to Dr. Ralph Heinicke for reviewing the manuscript and offering his feedback, and to Dr. Steven Hall for his review and feedback, and especially for writing the foreword to this book. And thank you Stephen and Aria Ray for your help, cooperation, and understanding while this book was being written.

Thank you to Valerie, who drew the illustrations, to Emily for her editorial suggestions and endorsement, to Beth for getting me started on Photoshop®, to Mark for his help with MSWord®, Pagemaker® and all our computer questions, and to Mac and Colby for being so easy to work with. Thank you also to the Hair Gallery and Salon in Marlborough, Connecticut for supplying some of the hair samples that I used in my research for the Noni Scalp Treatment.

By winter, 2000, my collection of Noni therapies grew to the point when a new edition of *"53 Ways"* seemed like a really good idea. A handful of very special individuals helped me give birth to *"76 Ways to Use Noni."* Thank you so much Ron Reid, Linda Upham, Val Dare, Sharlene King, Terese Malm, Belinda Dawson, Melech A. Franford, and McKinley Oswald.

FOREWORD

During the first half of this Century, a great deal of common-sense health care information was lost as our country went through the institutionalization and industrialization of medicine. This resulted in large segments of the population putting their care (along with their personal choices and power), into the hands of physicians, pharmaceutical companies, and technology. The second half of this Century, it seems, has been a reclaiming of our common-sense knowledge, personal choices, and personal power. This process of reclamation has come in waves, each wave growing as new waves developed.

The first wave was a growing awareness of the importance of good foods, then came the wave of vitamins and minerals, then the wave of phytonutrients (antioxidants, alkaloids, glucopolysaccharides, etc.), and herbs. I believe that Noni fruit juice exemplifies the crest of this latest wave. Phytonutrients represent a step beyond what we traditionally call "vitamins." They are specialized plant compounds that have beneficial functions in our bodies. Examples of good sources of phytonutrients you may already be familiar with include ginseng, licorice, ginkgo biloba, and aloe vera.

Noni fruit juice is known to contain many different kinds of phytonutrients. These include a glucopolysaccharide that is known to boost the immune system, a compound that inhibits viruses and cancerous changes in DNA, and the precursor to an alkaloid called xeronine that improves the functioning of your enzymes and cell wall receptors. These compounds work together to boost each other's effectiveness. And, they have been designed and formulated by the wisdom of nature rather than by someone in a laboratory. I have been working in the field of conventional, nutritional, and alternative medicine for twelve years and I have not seen another natural substance as interesting and widely effective as Noni fruit juice.

Optimal functioning of your immune system is vital to your overall wellness, every biochemical reaction in your body utilizes enzymes and all of your cellular communication mechanisms use cell wall receptors. Because Noni fruit juice works on such basic levels, you can well imagine that it has many uses. And, indeed, this is what we see clinically. I have used Noni fruit juice in my practice since October, 1996, and have seen dramatic results in hundreds of people. I have talked with yet hundreds more from all around the Country who are also seeing dramatic results from Noni fruit juice.

The concept of Noni fruit juice is simple. It is just a juice. And it is as safe for you as orange juice or apple juice. So how could it have so many powerful therapeutic benefits? After all, in our pharmacological culture, don't powerful therapies belong in the domain of physicians and aren't they known to have powerful side-effects? Can't people hurt themselves with a powerful therapy if they don't know what they are doing?

Generally, yes, but think about it this way. If you were severely deficient in vitamin C, you would have a condition called scurvy. Vitamin C, among other things, helps with the production of collagen, the main ingredient in our connective tissue. So scurvy is a condition where your body is literally falling apart. If you had scurvy, a glass of orange juice would have powerful therapeutic benefits. A glass or two of orange juice per day would prevent it altogether, and you would have to drink a tremendous amount of orange juice to hurt yourself.

The analogy applies to Noni in that many of us are severely xeronine deficient. Nutrient-depleted soils, environmental pollution, the stress of everyday life, aging, diseases, and certain food additives all work together to deplete our xeronine. Noni fruit juice supplies the necessary nutrients so that our bodies can make more xeronine.

As with other nutrients, herbs, or remedies, the more you know about Noni fruit juice, the more you can obtain its full benefits. This is the power and beauty of this book—that it can help you understand the wide range of applications of Noni fruit juice. When I first read *53 Ways to Use Noni Fruit Juice*, [now *76 Ways to Use Noni*], even after a year of using Noni fruit juice myself and in my practice, many of the concepts and applications were new to me. And I have to admit, I was somewhat skeptical. But I tried some of the suggestions myself and recommended others to patients and watched what happened. Now I am a believer.

I think that Isa Navarre has successfully synthesized intuitive and experimental science to bring us this straightforward yet comprehensive guide to the many uses of Noni fruit juice. I expect that this book will help you receive even more benefit from this juice, this amazing gift from God.

Steven M. Hall, M.D.
January 5, 1998

WHAT YOU SHOULD KNOW ABOUT NONI FRUIT JUICE

Since 1996, when Noni fruit juice first became commercially available, many Noni products have found their way to the marketplace. Most are powdered and in capsules and others are liquid. Of the liquid ones, some are the pure extract of the Noni fruit, and others are reconstituted from dried or powdered fruit. A few also contain extracts of the roots and leaves of the Noni plant.

In researching this book, I used juice that is a pure extract of the Noni fruit. It contains the perfect mix of the pulpy and the watery part of the fruit. This is important because these two fruit components have unique properties. Together, they are a dynamic pair.

I also feel it is important to know where the Noni that you use comes from. Noni grows in practically all tropical regions of the world, from Puerto Rico to India. However, the soils of the world simply aren't the same. The best Noni grows in unspoiled, nutrient rich soil—such as that of the remote Polynesian islands in the South Pacific. Juice from this fruit has unsurpassed purity and an abundance of healing compounds. Both these factors are critical to fully benefit from the applications in this book.

Please feel welcome to experiment with Noni fruit juice. Try a few of the procedures in this book. Customize them to suit your individual needs. Get to know Noni by finding out how your body responds to different dosages. Which topical applications help you the most?

Noni can become a life-long family friend. Read on, and allow me to introduce you...

INTRODUCTION

HOW MY EXPERIENCES
WITH NONI BEGAN:

"My cells remember this," I exclaimed moments after drinking my first ounce of Noni fruit juice. Somehow, Noni felt very familiar.

A few minutes later, changes started happening in my body. I was in my last month of pregnancy and the heartburn I had been suffering from subsided. I felt more calm and peaceful, and a tight muscle in my back suddenly released. I continued to take two ounces of Noni daily and the premature labor contractions I was having never came back. I was able to get out of bed and enjoy my last month of pregnancy walking around, working, and enjoying life.

Obviously, Noni was special. Of all the nutritional supplements I had tried over the years, nothing was as versatile and effective as Noni. I began to experiment with myself and my family, and was amazed at all the ways that Noni proved helpful.

Although it is better to take Noni on an empty stomach, the Noni Anti-acid Substitute, which is taken after a meal, did wonders for my indigestion. I also used Noni Massage Oil to help prevent stretch-marks and prepared Noni Tea to boost my immune system for the upcoming labor.

On October 30th, 1996, I gave birth to an eight-pound baby girl, named Aria Ray. My afterbirth cramps were very painful. Frequent Noni Compresses helped not only to reduce the pain, but also to heal the stitches I had received. A Trauma Dose sped my recovery, and a Maintenance Dose of two ounces a day helped me produce abundant milk to feed my baby.

Later, Noni Nose Drops cleared her stuffy nose. The Noni Tummy Treatment helped her body overcome a fever, and the Noni Rash Plaster quickly took care of an occasional diaper rash. Noni Ear Drops have helped all my children beat ear infections. The Noni Small Area Treatment and First Aid for Minor Wounds has helped everyone in my family. We have been amazed at how quickly Noni has sped our recovery from cuts, scrapes, burns, and scratches.

MY FAMILY'S MIRACLE:

In the summer of 1996, our German Shepherd dog, Aka, became severely ill. His hair fell out, and he scratched and chewed his body till it bled. Conventional treatment made him worse, and herbal and homeopathic remedies helped only a little.

In November, I tried giving him Noni. I followed the Procedure for Serious Conditions and every two weeks Interrupted Noni Therapy for a day or two. Twice a day I applied the Noni Topical Splash to his lesions. Five times a day, I used a plastic syringe to inject an ounce of Noni into his mouth.* He was very good about it. Maybe he knew it would help him feel better.

It did. By January he was completely healed. All his hair had grown back—in fact, it looked shinier and healthier than before. He also regained his playful joy for living.

Our whole family was so grateful for Noni!

*I used the 2:1 Dilution as described in my book, *Healing Secrets of Noni.*

WHY NONI WORKS:

Although this book focuses on the myriad ways to use Noni, I wanted to touch on why Noni works. Researchers have identified over one-hundred-fifty compounds in the *Morinda citrifolia*, or Noni fruit, that have therapeutic value.[1]

Two of these compounds* have been proven to be helpful against bacteria, fungus, inflammation, and allergies.[2] Another compound**, which is also found in essential oils, helps rejuvenate cells.[3] French scientists had success testing Noni's pain-killing elements.[4] Japanese researchers found a compound*** that inhibited pre-cancerous cells.[5] And Dr. Ralph Heinicke, of the University of Hawaii, discovered that Noni contains an appreciable quantity of a compound that he identified and named, "proxeronine."[6]

Proxeronine helps the body make an important alkaloid that Dr. Heinicke also discovered, which he called "xeronine." Xeronine is very important to the body because it regulates and strengthens the protein in our cells. Protein is found everywhere in our body and does many things. For example, proteins comprise the bulk of the organic material within the cell. Hemoglobin, insulin, collagen, as well as muscle and skin, cell membranes, blood vessel walls, blood clots, and many hormones are also made of protein.[7] Xeronine's impact on protein may help to explain Noni's effectiveness for so many different conditions.[8]

If you would like to read more about Noni's ingredients and studies which have been done on Noni, may I suggest the books, *Tahitian Noni Juice: How Much How Often for What*, by Neil Solomon, M.D. Ph.D.,[9] *Noni—Polynesia's Natural Pharmacy*,[10] and *Noni (Morinda citrifolia) Prize Herb of the South Pacific*.[11] These books are available from the company that distributes *76 Ways to Use Noni*.

*Anthraquinones and scopoletin

**Terpenes

***Damnacanthal

From 53 Ways to 76 Ways:

Soon after I was introduced to Noni fruit juice, I began recording the many ways I had found to use Noni. This resulted in the book, *53 Ways to Use Noni*. Since then, I have heard from Noni distributors around the world about how these techniques have helped them. They also offered new ideas for using Noni, which I added to my own growing repertoire. In November, 2000, I felt that I had gathered enough new "ways," that I could expand the book, and the publisher agreed. This edition, *76 Ways to Use Noni*, began to emerge.

In this edition, I wanted to offer a new paradigm for using Noni. I wanted to give people a breakthrough that would knock their socks off. Something really special. What I discovered surprised me for its simplicity and common sense: Incorporate Noni into a healthy lifestyle. Offer people ways to make Noni a Family Friend. Teach them to "Think Noni" as soon as a health concern arises. Give them a variety of Maintenance Dose procedures to choose from, so that taking Noni never gets boring and the Noni bottle never drifts to the back of the refrigerator.

People who are concerned about health invariably take nutritional supplements. The chapter, Taking Noni with Herbs and Supplements, tells how to best take Noni with supplements. The ills of dehydration and the body's need for enough water are health principles that are becoming increasingly recognized. Noni Maintenance Dose 4 and the Noni Procedure for Serious Conditions 2 each show a different way to take Noni with water. People are also becoming more aware of addictions and dependencies of all kinds. I like to think this coincides with our population's growing spiritual awareness, which is being reflected in physical-body awareness and resulting in a greater desire for freedom—including freedom from addictive substances. To support this growing trend, I have included ways that Noni can help people to quit smoking and become free of drugs, to eliminate the desire for alcohol, and to curb the clutches of food addictions.

This is just a sample of the new ways to use Noni that you will find in this book. There are also a few surprises in store: The Noni Chinese Body Clock Procedure marries Noni with a Chinese Medicine principle called the "body clock." This procedure can focus Noni's effects on a chosen organ. The chapter, Mixing Noni with Clay, introduces you to the wonders of a little-known, but remarkably therapeutic (and inexpensive) healing tool, which, like Noni, is also a gift of the earth. And the Noni Fast 3, which employs the principle of bio-rhythm, enables you to prompt a deep cleansing without having to restrict food intake.

How to Use
This Book:

I have divided the seventy-six ways to use Noni fruit juice that are described in this book into three sections. Section 1 covers different ways to drink Noni. Section 2 describes topical uses, and Section 3 covers techniques for taking Noni internally.

Each of the chapters in this book is also divided into three parts. In the first part, I suggest some conditions that might be helped by the Noni application that each chapter describes. This list is a guideline, and is not meant to provide medical advice or to be used as a prescription. If you have a condition that is not listed, but think the application might help, by all means try it. Of course, Noni won't always help everyone, even those who have conditions that are on the list.

In the second part of each chapter, I give detailed, step-by-step instructions on how to do each Noni application. Third, I offer some helpful information about the procedure.

At the back of this book, you'll find four appendices that attempt to address some of the questions people most often ask about Noni. The Health Evaluation Sheets in the first appendix are an invaluable tool for anyone looking to benefit from Noni. Appendix B contains information about cleansing reactions. Appendix C offers ideas why Noni may not work for you. Those who have found that

Noni has stopped working for them may find some possible explanations in Appendix D. I am very grateful to Dr. Ralph Heinicke for offering some additional insights into this topic.

In this edition I have made a few corrections to improve accuracy and readability. I have also added references to Noni Dilutions. Information about all fourteen Noni Dilutions, and their Harmonics, can be found in my book, *Healing Secrets of Noni.*

As you read this book, keep in mind that I am not a physician. The ideas that I offer for using Noni are not meant to replace your doctor's advice. I simply wanted to share what I know about Noni, and how my family and others have used Noni, so that you might have the opportunity to benefit as we have from this amazing and unique gift of nature.

A Gift Of Grace:

Occasionally in this book, I refer to Noni's "healing compounds." However, I do not believe that Noni itself heals. Health, and being healed of something, is a gift of Grace. Therapies and supplements, including Noni, simply give the body what it needs to receive these gifts. The applications in this book can help your body obtain all the blessings it can with the help of Noni.

Best wishes on your journey to greater health and well being!

Sincerely,
Isa Navarre
March, 2001

SECTION 1

DRINKING APPLICATIONS

Unlike juice beverages that we drink by the glassful, Noni fruit juice is taken in relatively small amounts. Most people drink it by the ounce (which equals only two tablespoonfuls). How many ounces of Noni is right for you depends on your health condition, and the way your body uniquely responds to Noni.

I am often asked how long it might take to notice beneficial effects from Noni. Some people notice health improvements almost immediately. A few must continue to take Noni for months before they enjoy significant results. But most people will notice a difference within a few weeks.

How much time your body will need to make the changes you want depends on many things. These factors include: how serious your condition is; how long you've had it; what other circumstances, stresses, or issues you are also dealing with, and what other therapies and supplements you may also be using. Noni might even enhance the benefits of these other therapies and supplements.

Section 1 offers a variety of techniques for drinking Noni, plus suggestions for acute, chronic, serious, and life-threatening health challenges. These are guidelines, which you may modify to suit your individual needs.

Every time I speak about Noni, someone inevitably asks me how to use Noni for such-and-such condition. I know many Noni enthusiasts also receive questions like this. Those who are not medical professionals cannot prescribe Noni. However we can refer people to the testimonials of others who have had similar afflictions. We can also ask people to describe their own condition: Is it acute, chronic, serious, or life-threatening? After they make this choice, we can refer them to the corresponding chapter in this book.

If you have several health challenges, select one to focus on first. Choose the procedure for taking Noni that best suits that challenge. Then try the topical and internal Noni applications that are appropriate for your condition. Continue with the applications and procedures you have chosen for at least three months. Your other health problems may also improve as a side-benefit.

If you are relatively healthy, or just have a few minor discomforts (nothing to write home about), a Maintenance Dose may be all that you need. If you are enjoying optimal health, the Top-Dose procedure may help fine-tune your body.

Section 1 has something for everyone, including children, teens and pets. Don't miss the chapter on Interrupting Noni Therapy, on page 39. And please try some of the Noni recipes on pages 119-124. My family tells me they're really good!

1.

YOUR
FIRST DOSE

Your adventure with Noni begins!

WHY YOU MIGHT
START TO TAKE NONI:

- To improve your overall health and well being.
- To boost your body's immune system.
- To take more responsibility for your health.
- To help your body heal after injury or surgery.
- To help support your body's natural healing processes.
- To better absorb the nutrients from your foods and from other supplements that you may be taking.

(cont.)

- To provide your body with certain nutrients that are not found in many foods today. One such nutrient is proxeronine, which is abundant in the Noni fruit.

- To try a natural approach to health and healing, because conventional methods that you have tried have not worked as well as you had expected.

- To strengthen your body's enzymes, cell receptor sites, and other cell proteins in order to help them work better.

- Your health care professional suggested that you try Noni.

- Noni helped a friend, who recommended that you try it too.

- You are a leader among your circle of friends, and often try new things first before recommending them to others.

How to Take
A First Dose:

1. Before you take your First Dose, fill out the Health Evaluation Sheet Part 1 in Appendix A (page 300). This will help you keep track of any changes that may occur after taking Noni. Also read the next chapter on "Evaluating the Immediate Effects of Noni." The information in that chapter can help you benefit the most from your first dose.

2. Turn the bottle of Noni fruit juice upside-down then right-side up a few times. This will mix the more watery part of the juice with the pulp, which tends to settle to the bottom of the bottle.

3. Open the bottle and pour out the desired amount of juice. Most people start with one ounce.

4. Sip about half the dose and hold it in your mouth for about ten seconds before swallowing. Do the same with the remainder of the dose.

EQUIVALENTS HELPFUL TO KNOW
FOR THE PROCEDURES IN THIS BOOK:

Three Teaspoonfuls = One Tablespoonful
Two Tablespoonfuls = One Ounce

MORE ABOUT
YOUR FIRST DOSE:

After a while, you will develop a style for drinking Noni. Some people measure the exact amount of Noni they want to take. Others pour into a glass an amount that seems "about right." Some just drink a few gulps a day straight from the bottle! However, if you are using Noni to help with a particular condition, try following the guidelines in this book.

To measure your Noni doses, you could use a tablespoon-sized measuring spoon. I use a one-ounce plastic medicine cup, which is much more convenient. Medicine cups are inexpensive, and you can find them in most drug stores. Larger doses of Noni can be measured in a glass measuring cup that lists liquid ounces. When you are measuring a liquid, hold the cup at eye level to ensure an accurate measurement.

Noni fruit juice is usually taken in one-tablespoonful or one-ounce doses. But start with one teaspoonful if you are less than five or six years old, or if you:

- Have a weak stomach.

- Are particularly sensitive to the effects of supplements.

- Are concerned that you might be among the rare few who are allergic to Noni or to the fruit juices that flavor it.

- Are concerned that Noni might cause an uncomfortable cleansing reaction.

(cont.)

5

- Are taking medications.
- Have heavy metal poisoning.
- Have severe toxicity.

If you have any of the above listed conditions, you may want to try the Procedure for Gradually Introducing Noni to the Body on page 81.

2.

EVALUATING THE IMMEDIATE EFFECTS OF NONI

Not everyone can sense Noni's effects right away. But this procedure is worth trying to see if you can. You may be surprised!

USE THIS PROCEDURE TO:

- Gain reassurance that Noni may help you.
- Discover how quickly Noni can begin to affect your body.
- Preview how and where Noni may help you first.
- Find out if your body will react unfavorably to Noni.
- Test your personal level of body awareness and sensitivity.

HOW TO EVALUATE
THE IMMEDIATE EFFECTS OF NONI:

1. Pour your first dose of Noni fruit juice.

2. Take a deep breath then exhale. This will give you a sense of your lung capacity. Look around the room at objects near and far, to sense the quality of your eyesight. This will give you two reference points with which to compare Noni's effects. Lung capacity and vision acuity are two body functions that are easy to self-evaluate, and that improve almost immediately when most people first take Noni.

3. Now sip about one-third to one-half of the dose, and hold the sip in your mouth for about ten to twenty seconds. Meanwhile, close your eyes and tune into any sensations you may be feeling in your body. Then swallow. Repeat with the remainder of the juice.

4. Examine how your body feels. Do you notice anything different?

   • Take another deep breath. Are your lungs able to take in more air, or is it easier to exhale without coughing? Do you feel more enlivened after taking a deep breath? Noni fruit juice is able to improve the body's ability to receive and use oxygen. Are your sinuses more open? Noni fruit juice acts as an anti-inflammatory agent.

   • Look around the room. Do things appear clearer; are colors more vivid? This is a common response, and may be due to Noni's effect on the pineal gland and neurotransmitter receptors. Noni fruit juice also helps the brain receive and translate information, including that which the eyes perceive.

   • Do you feel more calm and centered? Many people who live stressful lives find that Noni helps them relax.

   • Do you feel more energized? Noni fruit juice improves cellular function throughout the body.

   • Do you feel warmth anywhere in your body? Noni fruit juice may improve your circulation.

- If you have a particular health challenge, do you notice any difference in your symptoms? You may or may not notice changes so soon. Some people take Noni for weeks and sometimes months before they enjoy noticeable benefits.

- Do you feel more integrated throughout your body or a greater sense of connection with your Self? Noni helps the cells access information about their true purpose—information which may have become buried or obscured by disease or free radicals.

More about Evaluating The Immediate Effects of Noni:

It will be easier to notice differences in how you feel if you do this procedure with your first dose. If you try this procedure after you have already started taking Noni, the difference between how you feel before and after you take a dose probably won't be as obvious. Here's why. The first time you drink Noni, your level of health jumps to a higher plateau. Subsequent doses raise your level of health more gradually, or at a deeper level. Thus the changes are less obvious.

Moreover, when your body receives Noni for the first time, it may recognize that the Noni is filling a nutritional deficiency. You may feel better right away because unconsciously your body is trying to tell you, "Keep taking Noni. This is what I want and need!"

Changes in lung capacity and eyesight are easy for most people to notice. That is why I chose these two references for this procedure. Feel free to customize this procedure by changing or modifying the questions listed above, or the order in which you consider them.

Try using this procedure when you introduce Noni fruit juice to others. Lead them through each step as they take their first drink. This can be a fun way for friends to share Noni with each other. (See "Taking a First Dose with Others" on page 11.)

9

If, after taking your first dose, you have an immediate, uncomfortable reaction to Noni, it may be due to allergies, a cleansing reaction, or because your body is dehydrated. Allergies to Noni are probably very rare. But some people may be allergic to the fruit juices used to flavor the Noni fruit juice. Keep in mind that reactions that appear to be allergies may really be a cleansing. If you have a build-up of toxins that are ready to be released, taking one dose of Noni may be just enough to invite them out. (For more information on cleansing reactions and how to tell the difference between a cleansing reaction and an allergic reaction, see page 305-308.) For an explanation of how and why a dehydrated body can respond negatively to Noni, please read "More About the Noni Maintenance Dose 4," on pages 28 and 29.

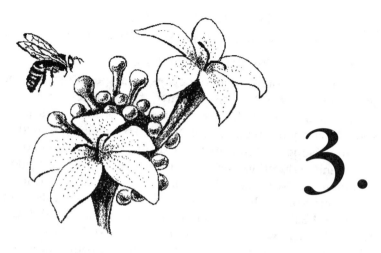

3.

TAKING A FIRST
DOSE WITH OTHERS

This method highlights the advantages of offering people a
first dose of Noni in a group environment.

INVITE PEOPLE TO TAKE
A FIRST DOSE WITH OTHERS:

- When you would like to offer your friends a supportive
  environment when taking their first dose.

- To maximize the enthusiasm and excitement that a group
  of people can feel when they share a common experience.

HOW TO INVITE PEOPLE
TO TAKE A FIRST DOSE WITH OTHERS:

1. Create a comfortable environment.

Invite your friends and associates to a special get-together that you might call a "Noni Party," "Noni Circle," or "Noni Experiential." Avoid the word "meeting" because it suggests something dry, boring, and long. You will be planning something fun, interesting, and informative that meets people's needs for community, education, enrichment, entertainment, and support.

Begin the Noni party by telling everyone how you found out about Noni. Talk about how you took your first dose and the first health improvements that you noticed. Tell your guests that you will soon invite them to try some Noni, to see who is naturally in-tune with it. Although Noni might have something to offer everyone, not everyone will feel its effects right away, although some do. You hope to provide an opportunity to find out if anyone present will have immediate effects—and have some fun at the same time.

If it feels right, tell your Noni business story too. If you are involved in distributing Noni, tell how you got involved in this facet of Noni. Do not underestimate the importance of your business story. It is something you started to write the moment you heard about Noni, and you add a new chapter with each level of success that you achieve. Your business story is your legacy. It should inspire others when they hear it, and yourself when you tell it.

After sharing your business story, get the focus back onto Noni fruit juice. Tell how Noni helped you in the weeks and months following your first dose. Then invite your associates who are also present, to tell their Noni stories too. Telling stories makes people feel comfortable and keeps their interest. It should also build a feeling of suspense, so that your guests can't wait to take their first drink of Noni.

> ### DON'T THINK YOU HAVE A NONI STORY?
> Ask yourself how Noni has helped you and your family. If Noni has helped you in any way, then you do indeed have a story to tell. Noni stories help people build an emotional connection to Noni. This is an essential key to sharing Noni with others. When someone has a heart connection to Noni, then conversations about Noni flow naturally.

2. Discuss Health Goals.

Go around the room and ask your guests what they hope to gain by taking Noni.

Then pass around Health Evaluation Sheets (page 300) and invite everyone to fill them out. This is a great opportunity for those who are already Noni enthusiasts to re-evaluate their progress towards greater health. If they have brought their old Evaluation Sheets, they can compare them with the one they fill out now, and relay their improvements to the group.

Show people your first Evaluation Sheet and subsequent ones. Show people how your symptoms have improved. This should help re-inspire you too! Working with the Evaluation Sheets will also build people's anticipation for taking their first dose. By-the-way, some people may want to keep their Evaluation Sheets private, and this desire should be respected.

3. Talk about how to take Noni and give directions for taking a first dose.

Show your guests the book, *76 Ways to Use Noni*, and talk about how easy it is to take Noni. Mention the maintenance doses and the other specific ways Noni can help for various conditions. Mention oral and topical applications. Share a few anecdotes.

Refer to page 8 and 9 in this book. Explain that, when taking a first dose, we like to follow the procedure outlined on those pages because it is the best way for people to notice Noni's effects as soon as possible. When people notice positive effects right away, they will naturally be very excited about improving their health with Noni.

4. Offer the first dose.

This is the highlight of the evening. Make the occasion special. Bring in enough wine glasses for everyone. Measure and pour an ounce of Noni into each glass. Then invite everyone to take their Noni—but one person at a time.

Decide who will take their dose first. Before they drink the Noni, remind them to put attention on their vision, their lung capacity, and their sense of calmness, vital energy, and well-being. Ask everyone else to pay attention. The group will watch and lend support as each person takes a dose. The group will also try to notice anything different about the person afterwards. Some changes may be dramatic enough that almost anyone can see them, like a change in posture, complexion, facial expression, and degree of relaxation. A few people might even be able to sense shifts in a person's energy after taking Noni.

After each individual takes a dose, ask for feedback about their Noni experience. What are they feeling? Can they sense what Noni is doing in their body or to which organ the Noni is going? Let them describe how their eyesight and lung capacity feels different. Ask the rest of the group to share the differences that they noticed too.

5. Listen, answer questions, and offer the next step.

When everyone has taken their dose, ask if anyone has any questions or comments about Noni. Listen attentively to each question and answer as best you can. Listening is important because people's confidence grows if they know they are being heard.

Finally, you want to tell everyone how they can get Noni on a regular basis. Some Noni distributors have trouble with this step because they don't want to feel as though they are "selling" something to their friends. Ideally, somebody will ask how to get more Noni, in which case you can tell them. (Or, beforehand, you may ask one of your close associates to ask this question in case nobody else does.)

Another way to prompt this question is to pass around a few copies of the book, *76 Ways to Use Noni*. Ask people which procedure they would like to try first—if they decided to take Noni regularly. To help them select a procedure, point out certain ones that might work best for their condition.

MORE ABOUT INVITING PEOPLE TO TAKE A FIRST DOSE WITH OTHERS:

This procedure provides an opportunity for people to discover Noni and to know within their heart if Noni is right for them. Without this heart connection, they won't be as committed to taking Noni. Those who believe in Noni not only become good customers, they also have a story to tell, and therefore have all the requisites to becoming reliable, committed distributors.

This procedure is ideal for a group that consists of people new to Noni plus those who are already Noni enthusiasts. However, you can modify these steps and follow them with only one or two other people to whom you are introducing Noni.

A big concern about introducing Noni to a group—or even to one person—is that they won't feel anything. Trust Noni and Trust Life. I think Noni chooses people more than people choose Noni. Try not to be attached to the outcome of whether or not someone will feel Noni's effects immediately or not. Know that those people who are meant to feel attuned to Noni will be. All you can do is provide the optimal environment for positive results, which is what this procedure is designed to do.

If someone says, "I don't feel anything." Tell them, "Okay, let's wait a few minutes, let someone else have a turn, and then we'll check back with you." It may take a few minutes for that person's body to respond to Noni. Or it may take a few weeks.

There will always be people who ask the hard questions. They may be skeptical, but they are also willing to be convinced. After all, they did show up for the meeting, didn't they? So they are not as closed-minded as they may sound. If Noni does indeed work for these people, they are likely to become loyal Noni enthusiasts.

Many people experience immediate effects after taking Noni.

When they have the opportunity to experience these effects in a group—with all the support and community around them—the excitement for Noni can become unbelievable.

The steps in this procedure are designed to build suspense and enthusiasm for Noni. As these feelings grow during the evening, the more excited and open people will be. The less likely they will be to say "I don't feel anything," and the more likely they will be to say, "Wow, this Noni is fantastic!"

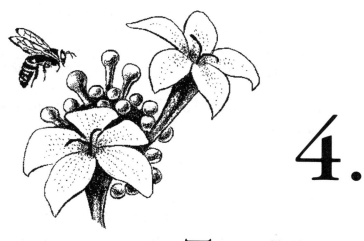

4.

THE NONI
MAINTENANCE
DOSE 1

Ah, the plain old daily dose...

TAKE THE NONI
MAINTENANCE DOSE 1 WHEN:

- You are relatively healthy and have only minor health challenges or none at all.
- You know that Noni supplies important nutrients, and just want to take enough Noni to cover your daily needs.

(cont.)

- You are between cycles of more vigorous Noni therapy, such as the Top Dose Procedure (page 35).

- Another Noni therapy has alleviated a particular condition, and it is time to reduce the amount of Noni you are taking.

- You are not trying to test Noni's potential or its effectiveness.

- You have diabetes.

HOW TO TAKE
THE NONI MAINTENANCE DOSE 1:

HOW MUCH IS A MAINTENANCE DOSE?

- A Maintenance Dose for the average adult is one ounce of Noni fruit juice per day.

- Adults who are overweight may also take one ounce per day. They need not take extra Noni to compensate for their excess weight.

- Adults who have large frames, but who are not overweight, may try two ounces of the juice per day as maintenance.

- Adults who weigh less than one hundred pounds may use a Maintenance Dose of one tablespoonful of Noni per day.

- See also "Giving Noni to Children" on page 125.

If your Maintenance Dose is one ounce or less of Noni per day:

Drink your entire Maintenance Dose upon awakening. Take it at least a few minutes before you eat, smoke, or drink anything else but water.

If your Maintenance Dose is two ounces of Noni per day:

Drink one ounce upon awakening. Take the other ounce that afternoon or evening, preferably on an empty stomach.

MORE ABOUT
THE NONI MAINTENANCE DOSE 1:

The Maintenance Dose may be Sipped, (page 43) or swallowed All-at-Once (page 45), whichever you prefer.

A Maintenance Dose is meant to supply enough of Noni's healing compounds, such as proxeronine, to meet the body's daily needs. On days of unusual stress, these needs will increase. Double or triple your Maintenance Dose on these occasions.

For the first couple of months that you are on the Maintenance program, consider doubling the suggested Maintenance Dose. This will help correct any deficiencies that you may have in Noni's micronutrients. A morning dose of Noni taken upon awakening may help you overcome the need for a morning cigarette or cup of coffee. Many people can testify, through personal experience, how Noni has helped them overcome addictions. (See Noni Quit-Smoking Techniques on page 89.) If necessary, prepare your morning dose the night before and put it beside your bed. This way, it becomes the first thing you reach for each morning.

Taking Noni on an empty stomach can cause discomfort in some people. This is because Noni's cleansing effect often works on the stomach first. This is especially true if the individual has a stomach condition, or any degree of toxicity there. For example, one morning I awoke with an undigested meal still in my stomach. My morning dose of Noni gave me an acid feeling. But this soon passed, and by-the-way, I didn't feel lethargic that day as I usually do after eating such a heavy meal the night before.

If your morning dose of Noni causes discomfort, for any reason, try reducing that dose on following mornings. Compensate by taking more Noni for your afternoon or evening dose. You may also try one of the other Noni Maintenance Dose procedures in this book, in particular, Noni Maintenance Dose 4 (see page 27).

After you have taken the Maintenance Dose for a few months, try Interrupting Noni Therapy (page 39) for a few days. Do this every three or four months. Interrupting Noni Therapy may improve your body's ability to receive Noni's benefits, and will keep Noni working to your best advantage.

The Maintenance Dose is ideal for diabetics because of the ability for only one or two ounces of Noni per day to lower blood sugar levels. Because this can happen in a relatively short period of time, diabetics should pay extra attention to their blood sugar level while taking Noni fruit juice. Those who don't monitor their sugar level and adjust their insulin intake as needed, could experience insulin shock. This is a loss of consciousness that is caused by an overdose of insulin.

Diabetics can modify the Maintenance Dose procedure by taking one tablespoonful of Noni a few minutes before each meal. Assuming a diet of three meals daily, this would amount to one-and-a-half ounces of Noni a day.

Insulin-dependent diabetics should take no more than two ounces of Noni a day for the first few weeks. In the meantime, they should monitor their blood sugar level to find out how Noni affects them. Then, if they want stronger results, they can gradually increase the amount of Noni they take to one ounce per dose (or three ounces of Noni a day).

Children with diabetes can start with one teaspoonful of Noni before each meal. Older children can try two teaspoonfuls.

Many topical and internal Noni applications, described in Sections 2 and 3 of this book, can be helpful to address the various other symptoms common to diabetes.

5.

THE NONI
MAINTENANCE
DOSE 2

Some people get locked into the habit of taking only a certain number of ounces of Noni daily. The Maintenance Dose 2 provides a basis for being more flexible with Noni. Hopefully, it will make people feel more at ease to vary the amount of Noni they take each day.

TRY THE NONI MAINTENANCE DOSE 2 WHEN:

- You are relatively healthy and have only minor health challenges or none at all.
- You have been taking the Noni Maintenance Dose 1 for a while.

- You have suddenly been faced with new challenges, changes or stress.
- The Maintenance Dose that you have been taking doesn't seem to be giving you the same support as before.
- You have a degree of comfort with and confidence in taking Noni fruit juice.

How to take the Noni Maintenance Dose 2:

Every so often, or when you think you need to:

- Take more Noni fruit juice than you usually do. Take two ounces instead of one. Or three ounces instead of two.
- For a few days, try taking less Noni fruit juice than you usually do. For example, if you usually take two or three ounces daily, try taking just one ounce.
- Try Interrupting Noni Therapy (page 39).
- Sip your doses of Noni (page 43) instead of drinking them All-at-Once (page 45), or vice versa.
- Vary your doses for a week or two. Play with the Technique for Stubborn Conditions (page 77).
- Try other creative ways to take Noni that you might think of.
- Keep Noni a Family Friend (page 129).

More About the Noni Maintenance Dose 2:

The underlying philosophy of the Maintenance Dose 2 is to pay attention to how Noni is helping you and don't make a habit of taking the same dose all the time. Feel free to experiment. Remember that an attitude of creativity and flexibility, and a willingness to try new things makes the body more receptive to heath and healing.

The Noni Maintenance Dose 2 has no hard, fast rules. It is meant to remind you to be flexible with Noni. Change is a constant in our lives, and Noni will be there to help—especially if we can learn to modify the way we use Noni to meet our changing needs.

6.

THE NONI
MAINTENANCE
DOSE 3

The Noni Maintenance Dose 3 includes many elements of good health including relaxation, deep breathing, meditation, creative visualization, "letting go," exercising gratitude, and drinking Noni. Together, they elevate the "plain old" Maintenance Dose into a powerful healing regimen.

TRY THE NONI MAINTENANCE DOSE 3 WHEN:

- You have been taking other Noni Maintenance Dose procedures for a while.

- You would like to try a new approach to using Noni for health maintenance.

How to take
The Noni Maintenance Dose 3:

1. Find ten minutes in your daily schedule when you can routinely take your Noni. Ideally, it should be at the same time every day and also at a time when the house is quiet and you can be alone.

2. Measure the amount of Noni that you want to take, and pour it into a glass.

3. Find a comfortable place to sit, with your Noni nearby.

4. Close your eyes, relax, and take three long, deep breaths. Let your worries slip away on each exhale. Breathe in new life and vitality on each inhale. Try to visualize stress and tension leaving your body when you exhale, and youthful energy entering your body on the inhale.

5. Open your eyes and take a sip of Noni.

6. Repeat Steps 4 and 5 until your dose is finished. Take as much time as you want. Meanwhile, nurture a feeling of gratitude for Noni, for your body, and for your health.

ALSO TRY THIS PROCEDURE FOR SERIOUS CONDITIONS.

This Noni technique is suggested as a maintenance dose in order to encourage people to use it regularly. However, it can be especially helpful for any condition including serious ones. No matter which other Noni procedures you may be using, you can follow the steps outlined in this chapter at least once a day.

MORE ABOUT
THE NONI MAINTENANCE DOSE 3:

Nurturing gratitude and love for oneself and one's body, as suggested in Step 6, is another powerful way to rejuvenate and reduce stress. Try giving attention to each part of your body and feeling gratitude for it. If certain parts are not working as they should be, send them healing energy by feeling love and gratitude for them.

The method for taking Noni outlined in this chapter can be applied to other procedures for taking Noni. It may be especially helpful for those with serious conditions or conditions where the ailing organs can be pinpointed. Then, in Step 6, you can focus healing love and gratitude on that particular organ.

If your usual maintenance dose regimen includes taking Noni twice a day, you could combine both doses into one when you follow this procedure. Or follow this procedure with one dose and take the other as you normally would. Of course, if you have the time, you can do this procedure with both doses.

Breathing deeply before taking Noni opens pathways for Noni's healing compounds to reach more cells and more deeply into the cells than regular breathing. The extra oxygen brought into the body may also enhance the effects of these compounds.

If you do not have time to follow all the steps in this procedure, at least take a few deep breaths before drinking your Noni doses.

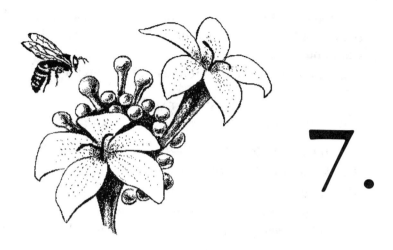

7.

THE NONI MAINTENANCE DOSE 4

If you feel discomfort after taking Noni fruit juice, such as an upset stomach, light-headedness, or other cleansing reactions, here is a way to take Noni that may allow your body to accept Noni more easily.

TRY THE NONI MAINTENANCE DOSE 4 WHEN:

- You are prone to cleansing reactions.
- You have a sensitive constitution.
- Your stomach easily gets upset.
- You have tried Noni before and had an aversion to it.
  (cont.)

- You have health challenges that indicate taking several ounces of Noni a day, but your body (or your pocketbook) can handle only one or two.
- You do not drink eight to ten glasses of water a day.

How to take
The Noni Maintenance Dose 4:

1. Fill an eight- to ten-ounce glass with purified water.
2. Drink about half the glass of water.
3. Take a tablespoonful of Noni fruit juice.
4. Drink the rest of the water in the glass.

Figure out how many times you have to do Steps 1 through 4 each day:

a. First decide how many ounces of Noni you would like to take per day.

b. Then multiply this number by two. The answer you get will be the number of tablespoonfuls of Noni to take daily. (There are two tablespoonfuls in every ounce.) For example, if you would like to take two ounces of Noni a day, you will be taking four table-spoonfuls of Noni, and will have to follow the procedure above four times daily.

More about
The Noni Maintenance Dose 4:

Drinking water before taking Noni does two things. First, it lubricates the body and provides a pathway for Noni's healing compounds to reach and enter the cells that need them. Second, it satisfies thirsty cells. Dehydrated cells actually take in more Noni healing compounds than they should. As the cells drink in the liquid that Noni fruit juice provides, they also take in Noni healing compounds. If they take in more compounds than they can process with their limited supply of water, bio-chemical imbalances can occur. The symptoms that result can seem like a cleansing or allergic reaction, but are really evidence of this bio-chemical imbalance. This is why people who are dehydrated tend to have a natural aversion to Noni. Either it tastes repulsive or they feel worse rather than better after trying a dose or two. This occurs because the brain knows that the body does not have enough water to distribute Noni properly, or that Noni may flood certain cells with more healing compounds than they can handle. The brain knows that the body needs to satisfy its need for water first. Only then it can take full advantage of Noni's healing compounds.

Drinking water immediately after taking Noni dilutes the Noni, so that it can disperse more freely throughout the body instead of pooling in the esophagus or stomach.

You may wonder, what is the difference between drinking water before and after taking Noni, verses adding the Noni to the water and then drinking it as a mixture (as suggested in the Noni Procedure for Serious Conditions 2, page 69). The important difference is that the body receives Noni undiluted. Undiluted Noni can shock the body into a healing mode, whereas drinking Noni added to a glass of water does not.

The presence of undiluted Noni on the tongue tells the brain that a significant healing substance is now inside the body. The brain cannot ignore undiluted Noni. If the body is functioning as it should and is well-enough hydrated, the brain will respond by signalling which cells should receive Noni's healing compounds. It will also help distribute the Noni around the body as needed. Noni Maintenance 4 gives you all the benefits of taking Noni undiluted, plus it gives the body the water it needs to get the most and the best from Noni's healing compounds.

For a further comparison of taking Noni undiluted or mixed with water, please read, More About the Noni Procedure for Serious Conditions 2, on pages 70-72.

The Noni Maintenance Dose 4 is preferred over other Noni Maintenance procedures if the body is dehydrated to any degree. Again, if the body is dehydrated, it may reject Noni. It can do this through a repulsive taste, nausea, rashes, diarrhea, and other symptoms.

8.

Taking Noni with Herbs and Supplements

A reminder about something that may seem obvious.

Take Noni
With Other Supplements:

- As part of your daily routine.
- To get the maximum benefit from other supplements that you may be taking.

How to Take Noni
with Other Supplements:

1. Measure the dose of Noni that you want to take.

2. Gather the other supplements that you want to take. These can include vitamins, minerals, herbs, and anti-oxidants. Also fill a glass with purified water, to help you take these supplements.

3. Drink your dose of Noni. Immediately afterwards, take the supplements.

More About
Taking Noni with Other Supplements:

Recently, a leading international Noni fruit juice bottling company and exporter began to produce a highly concentrated form of Noni, which they combined with other herbs. They discovered that Noni's healing compounds naturally complement an herb's healing properties. Moreover, Noni is a highly effective delivery system.[12] This means that Noni helps herbs react more favorably to the human body. Noni has also been found to enhance the effects of medications, so that less medication may be needed.[13] These findings suggest that Noni may be able to enhance the effectiveness of any nutritional supplement, simply because it makes the body better prepared to receive it.

However, do not reduce the amount of supplements that you take without consulting your health-care provider. There is no way to know how well Noni improves your body's unique ability to absorb supplements. In most cases, the excess supplements your body does not need will be passed out in the urine.

The dose of Noni that you take with supplements should be counted among the doses of Noni that you take each day. In other words, you do not have to take extra Noni when taking it with supplements.

Because you will be taking Noni immediately before drinking water and taking your supplements, the water you drink should be pure. Use distilled water, spring water, purified tap water, or clean-and-untreated well water. Chlorine, fluorine, or other chemicals used to treat tap water will interfere with the body's ability to absorb and use Noni's healing compounds.

Also, try adding Noni to herbal teas, herbal poultices, and herbal baths. Add up to one tablespoonful of Noni to a cup of tea. Add as much as two or three ounces of Noni to herbal poultices or baths. Use your judgement about how much Noni to add to herbs based on the quantity of herbs used and the size of the area to be covered.

Herbal tinctures are best mixed with Noni rather than taking the two separately. Add one dropperful of herbal tincture to one ounce of Noni fruit juice. Gently stir the two liquids together to combine them. Take this dosage two to five times a day, depending on the severity of your condition.

Noni fruit juice can also be mixed with other medicinal fruit extracts such as Saw Palmetto Berry extract and Hawthorne Berry extract. Mix one dropperful of extract with one ounce of Noni, as described in the previous paragraph. Saw Palmetto Berry extract is traditionally used for prostate conditions. By itself, Noni does not reach the prostate gland as effectively as it does when combined with Saw Palmetto, which draws Noni's healing compounds to that area. Hawthorne Berry is traditionally used for heart conditions, and can focus Noni's healing compounds in the heart tissue.

Undiluted Noni can also be mixed with garlic to help lower cholesterol levels—a traditional use of garlic. Both the garlic and Noni tend to potentize each other. To try this combination: mix one clove of crushed (not chopped) garlic per ounce of Noni fruit juice. Allow the mixture to rest in the refrigerator a few hours or overnight. Strain the garlic pieces. Then drink a tablespoonful of this mixture at least once a day. Take this mixture in addition to other doses of Noni that you may already be taking. If you find the taste of the Noni-garlic mixture too strong by itself, try adding it to other foods. It tastes delicious with a little olive oil, over salad.

I have also found that Noni fruit juice does not interfere with homeopathic remedies. On the contrary, taking Noni about fifteen minutes before taking a homeopathic remedy seems to enhance the remedy's effects.

In addition, many Noni enthusiasts are having a great deal of success combining Noni with inositol, a vitamin in the B complex. They have used it to alleviate the symptoms of a variety of conditions including diabetes, multiple sclerosis, arthritis, and severe nerve pain.

9.

The Noni
Top Dose
Procedure

If you are relatively healthy, here is a way to find out how much Noni your body needs to make significant changes in your health.

When to try the
Top Dose Procedure:

Try the Top Dose Procedure if you have the physical constitution to handle a possibly intense cleansing, and if you are:

- Experiencing systemic toxicity, yeast, or parasites.

(cont.)

- Experiencing a new health challenge, and want to address it before it becomes chronic.
  - In top physical condition and want to see if Noni can:
    - Fine-tune your body.
    - Improve your performance.
    - Take you to a new level of health.
    - Increase your strength, stamina, and endurance.
    - Build extra muscle or improve the quality of the muscle tissue you already have.
- A health-care professional who wants to evaluate the potential of Noni personally before offering it to patients.
- An athlete who wants to evaluate how Noni can enhance his or her performance.

HOW TO FIND
YOUR TOP DOSE:

Before you begin, fill out the Health Evaluation Sheet Part 1 in Appendix A (page 300). This will help you spot minor health improvements, which may otherwise go unnoticed.

Plan to keep track of how much Noni you take each day by marking the amount on a calendar. Also, each day record how you feel and any changes in your health—even minor ones. This way, you can look back to see how much Noni you were taking when any improvements occurred. It will also help you identify your Top Dose.

1. For three days, take one ounce of Noni each day.

2. For the next three days, take two ounces of Noni a day. Take one ounce upon awakening and the other in the afternoon or evening, preferably on an empty stomach.

3. Every three days, increase your daily dose either by one tablespoonful or one ounce.

4. Stop increasing your dose when:
   - Your physical performance reaches a new plateau.

- Your general sense of well-being or mental clarity improves significantly.

- A symptom that has been bothering you improves significantly.

This dose is your "Top Dose."
However:

- At the first sign of a cleansing reaction (pages 305-308),

- Or, if you sense that you are taking more Noni than your body can handle,

Go back to the dose you were taking before you last increased it. This dose will be your "Top Dose."

Take this dose even if cleansing symptoms continue. When the cleansing is over, you should notice improvements in your physical, emotional, or mental health and well being.

5. Continue to take your Top Dose daily for a couple of weeks. Take it longer if you are very physically active.

6. Then Interrupt Noni Therapy (page 39) for several days.

7. Repeat Steps 1 through 6 when you are ready for another cycle of active health improvement.

MORE ABOUT THE
TOP DOSE PROCEDURE:

The first time you do this procedure, your Top Dose may be as little as two or three ounces a day, or it may be as much as eight or twelve ounces a day. If your Top Dose is large, your body could have a great need for Noni's healing compounds. Or, if you are in optimal condition, it may take a lot of Noni to bring on a cleansing reaction or put you into a healing mode, which would eventually improve your health even more.

The next time you do this procedure, your Top Dose may be different if your body's needs have changed.

The Top Dose Procedure may be repeated continually. But it is not recommended unless you are physically, mentally, and emotionally prepared for change. The Top Dose Procedure challenges the body to a new level of health. This may naturally involve a cleansing on many levels. Please read about cleansing reactions (page 305) before you decide to do this procedure.

Another option is to do the Top Dose Procedure twice a year, for example, in Spring and Autumn. Doing so would support the body's natural cleansing cycles during these seasons.

If you are doing the Top Dose Procedure to evaluate Noni fruit juice, also experiment with other topical and internal Noni applications described in this book. A fair test of any health product, is to take it for at least three months.

10.

Interrupting Noni Therapy

Noni fruit juice can be a life-long friend. But every so often it can be helpful to stop taking Noni for short periods of time. Then, once you start taking Noni again, you may feel better than you did before.

Try Interrupting Noni Therapy When:

- Conditions that Noni fruit juice once alleviated have returned.
- Noni is not helping a condition as much as you think it should.
- Your health has improved to a plateau, and doesn't seem to be getting any better.
- You have been using Noni daily for a while, and now it is time to give your body a rest, to honor the natural cycles of healing.

- You want to avoid becoming accustomed to Noni, so that you don't have to keep increasing your doses to get the same results.

- You want to evaluate how well Noni is working for you, by comparing your condition when taking, and when not taking Noni.

- You want to stimulate the body into a healing mode.

- You want to encourage your cells to use Noni's healing compounds more effectively and efficiently.

- Also, pregnant mothers may consider Interrupting Noni Therapy for one week a month during their second and third trimesters. This would eliminate any possibility, however remote, that their baby might be born desensitized, or even allergic to, certain Noni healing compounds.

HOW TO
INTERRUPT NONI THERAPY:

1. Take Noni fruit juice for about two to three months.

2. Then stop taking it for two to seven days.

3. Start taking Noni again, only this time the dosage you need may be lower than what you took before.

MORE ABOUT
INTERRUPTING NONI THERAPY:

Interrupting Noni Therapy should be done every few months, as long as you use Noni fruit juice.

However, do not Interrupt Noni Therapy if you have immune deficiency conditions, diabetes, or cancer. These conditions require Noni's constant support.

- In the case of immune deficiency conditions, Noni's healing compounds lead the immune system on a course of steady but gradual improvement. Withdrawing this support may cause the immune system to lose too much ground on its progress towards greater health.

- In the case of cancer, pain may return and tumors that have stopped growing may start to grow back.[14]

- With diabetes, Noni's healing compounds may help stabilize blood sugar levels. Withdrawing Noni could cause unnecessary swings in the body's chemistry.

> If you have a serious health challenge and symptoms return while you are Interrupting Noni Therapy, start again on Noni immediately. Also, be sure to inform your physician.

How long should you Interrupt Noni Therapy? In general, those who have health challenges might stop taking Noni for only two to three days. Those who are generally healthy may abstain from Noni for as long as a week.

When deciding how long to Interrupt Noni Therapy, also consider:

- How serious your health challenges are.

- How well Noni has been helping you so far.

- How you feel when you don't take Noni.

If Noni doesn't seem to be helping auto-immune conditions (conditions in which the immune system is attacking the body as if it were foreign), Interrupt Noni Therapy for relatively short intervals of one or two days. Try this as often as every two or three weeks.

Another testimony to Noni's truly amazing properties, is its ability to affect the healing cycle. The healing cycle consists of alternating phases of rest, and phases in which healing changes take place. Both parts of the cycle are essential to make lasting improvements in the body's health.

Interrupting Noni Therapy initiates a rest phase in the healing cycle. Reintroducing Noni jump-starts the body into the phase where it makes positive change. Removing Noni from the diet may also prompt the cells to recognize that they cannot rely on

a steady supply of Noni healing compounds. When Noni is rein-
troduced, the cells may better appreciate these healing compounds, and use them more effectively and efficiently.

Interrupting Noni Therapy is discussed further in
Appendix D on page 319.

11.

SIPPING NONI

Here is one of several techniques for drinking your Noni doses.

TRY SIPPING FOR:

- Acute* conditions.
- Acute pain (after you have taken a Trauma Dose).
- Chronic** pain, to enhance the effects of the Procedure for Chronic Conditions.
- Conditions in which swallowing is difficult.
- Extreme illness.
- Overcoming cravings for nicotine or other addictive substances.

*Acute conditions are short-lived, usually start quickly, and are relatively severe.
**Chronic conditions last for a long time, or recur frequently.

How to Sip
Noni Fruit Juice:

1. Pour your dose of Noni fruit juice into a cup.

2. Take a small quantity of the juice and hold it in your mouth for a few seconds before swallowing. Separate each sip by at least a few seconds, and for as long as a few minutes.

3. Repeat Step 2 until the dose is gone.

More about
Sipping Noni Fruit Juice:

Instead of sipping Noni from a cup, you can sip it through a straw. Straws are especially convenient for taking Noni when you cannot sit up. If you have trouble swallowing, have someone give you the Noni with an eyedropper.

If you want to Sip Noni while at work, bring your Noni in a thermos. This will keep the juice fresh.

For some people, Sipping their Noni alleviates pain more effectively than taking a full dose of juice All-at-Once, as described in the following chapter. Of course, others find that drinking a dose of Noni All-at-Once is more helpful. Experiment to see which method works best for you.

12.

DRINKING NONI
ALL-AT-ONCE

"Cheers!"

WHEN TO DRINK
NONI ALL-AT-ONCE:

- For a boost of energy.
- For pain.
- For relatively minor injuries.
- To help wake up in the morning.
- To jump start the body into a phase of positive change in the healing cycle.
- To quickly raise the body's level of health.
- When taking the Trauma Dose.

How to Drink
Noni All-at-Once:

1. Pour your dose of Noni fruit juice into a cup.

2. Drink the dose in one or two large swallows, without stopping for breath.

More about
Drinking Noni All-at-Once:

Drinking a dose without stopping for breath is not as hard as it may sound. Most Noni doses are comprised of only one or two ounces of liquid. Of course, if you are physically unable to drink Noni All-at-Once, then just drink it as fast as you can.

If you are taking a relatively large dose of Noni, such as the Trauma Dose (which is about one-half cup of Noni), you may have to swallow once or twice to drink the entire dose.

When taking Noni fruit juice for pain, try drinking your first dose All-at-Once, and then Sipping subsequent doses.

Drinking Noni All-at-Once is most effective if you take the Noni on an empty stomach. The presence of food in the stomach can interfere with the Noni's ability to "shock" the body into the active phase of the healing cycle. This is the phase in which positive changes are made. (For more information about the healing cycle, see page 41.)

13.

THE AUTO-
DILUTION

When Noni fruit juice is held under the tongue, it will mix with a certain amount of saliva. The resulting mixture forms an "Auto-dilution," a custom-made remedy tailored to the body's current needs.

TRY THE AUTO-DILUTION
FOR CONDITIONS SUCH AS:

- Auto-immune diseases.
- Biochemical imbalances.
- Chronic Fatigue Syndrome.
- Depression

    (cont.)

- Eating disorders.
- Emotional stress.
- Extreme fatigue.
- Grief.
- Low energy and vitality.
- Mental illness.
- Profound sadness.
- Trauma (after taking a Trauma Dose).

How to do
The Auto-dilution:

1. Hold a small sip of Noni fruit juice in your mouth underneath your tongue.

   Make sure the top of your tongue is up against the roof of your mouth. Put the front of your tongue against the back of your lower front teeth. This is a natural position for your tongue, and it will help to seal the Noni underneath your tongue. Saliva will naturally mix with the Noni, and some of this mixture will naturally be swallowed.

2. After a few minutes, swallow all the Noni-saliva mixture. You may do this gradually, or with one swallow.

More about
The Auto-Dilution:

The Auto-dilution procedure may be used as often as you like. You could even drink all of your Noni doses this way.

It is easier to hold the Noni in your mouth when your attention is involved with something else. One idea is to do the Auto-dilution while taking a shower. Then you may be able to hold the Noni in your mouth for a longer period of time, because you will be less distracted.

After taking the Auto-dilution, you may feel more centered with greater emotional calmness, and have increased energy, vitality, and alertness.

The Auto-dilution may affect your appetite, according to your body's needs. For example, if Noni increases your appetite, you may be deficient in one or more nutrients. The Noni is simply telling your body to eat more in order to obtain these nutrients. Try a full spectrum nutritional supplement, and the food cravings should go away. On the other hand, the Auto-dilution may decrease your appetite if you have been eating too much or if your body is ready to lose some weight.

The Auto-dilution is the best way for someone who is debilitated with illness to take Noni. Use an eyedropper to place a small amount of Noni under the person's tongue.

The Auto-dilution can be used as the Noni equivalent of the homeopathic Rescue Remedy®.

If you have a serious condition located in your head or brain, take extra care to hold your tongue securely against the roof of your mouth. If Noni makes prolonged contact with the roof of your mouth, it can draw toxins from the head through the soft palate. In this case, the Noni should be spit out. See The Oral Detox Procedure, which is described in the next chapter.

If you have amalgam fillings in your teeth that are causing symptoms of mercury poisoning, do not use the Auto-dilution technique. Try the Oral Detox instead.

14.

THE ORAL DETOX

When Noni is held in prolonged contact with the roof of the mouth, it is possible to draw toxins out of the head and brain.

TRY THE ORAL DETOX FOR:

Conditions in the mouth, head, and brain including:

- Cancer.
- Headaches.
- Mental Illness.
- Mercury poisoning or chemical toxicity.
- Overcoming cravings for nicotine, caffeine, and other addictive substances.

How to do
The Oral Detox:

1. Take a small sip of Noni fruit juice.

2. Trap the Noni on top of your tongue and against the roof of your mouth by gently pressing the edges of your tongue against the inside of your upper teeth. This will also discourage saliva from mixing with the Noni, although some inevitably will. Hold the sip in your mouth for about 30 to 60 seconds.

3. Then spit out the Noni.

4. Rinse your mouth with purified water.

More about
The Oral Detox:

Avoid swallowing the Noni. If your mouth produces too much saliva to avoid swallowing, or if the Noni drips down your throat, spit some of it out. This will reduce the volume of liquid in your mouth. Next time take a smaller sip. Too much saliva mixed with the Noni will reduce the effectiveness of the Oral Detox procedure.

Even though it is suggested that you hold the Noni against the roof of your mouth for 30 to 60 seconds, spit out the Noni sooner if you feel light-headed or have any other cleansing reaction.

Start by doing the Oral Detox once a day for about a week. Then try it twice a day if you are feeling well and think you can handle a stronger detoxification.

Do not underestimate the cleansing potential of the Oral Detox. If detoxification happens too quickly, you may get a headache or experience other cleansing symptoms. Drink plenty of purified water to help flush the toxins from your body. For other ideas about what to do during cleansing, refer to Appendix B, "Cleansing Reactions," on page 305.

THE DIFFERENCE BETWEEN

THE ORAL DETOX AND THE AUTO-DILUTION

In the Oral Detox, Noni is held on top of the tongue. The purpose of the Oral Detox is to pull toxins from out of the head.

In the Auto-dilution, Noni is held underneath the tongue. The purpose of the Auto-dilution is to adapt the vibrational signature of the Noni to match the individual's condition at a given time. Like a homeopathic remedy, the Auto-dilution can then help to normalize the condition, and return harmony to the individual.

If the Oral Detox causes too strong a cleansing reaction, do the Oral Detox less frequently, perhaps only once every other day. Or, continue to do the Oral Detox daily with the following change: Instead of taking a sip of Noni straight from the bottle, use a special mixture of purified water and Noni fruit juice that I call the 1:8 Dilution*. To make this mixture:

1. Pour an ounce of Noni fruit juice into a pint-size jar.

2. Measure eight ounces (one cup) of purified water in a measuring cup.

3. Pour the water into the jar in a steady, uninterrupted stream. Meanwhile, swirl the jar for several seconds to mix the liquids together.

4. Take a sip from this mixture to do the Oral Detox.

5. Store the unused Noni-water mixture in the refrigerator.

Wait about half a day after doing the Oral Detox before drinking a dose of Noni. You want to ensure that any cleansing reactions brought on by the Oral Detox have a chance to run their course.

The Oral Detox may ease head and mouth pain. It may also contribute to increased mental clarity and improved

*All fourteen Noni Dilutions are described in my book, *Healing Secrets of Noni.*

memory. Other beneficial "side-effects" may include relief from conditions such as gingivitis, toothache, mouth infections, and sores.

15.

A PROCEDURE FOR ACUTE CONDITIONS

This procedure is designed for acute* conditions that are not serious or life threatening. Or, when you first experience symptoms of what you suspect may become a chronic condition.

TRY THIS PROCEDURE
FOR CONDITIONS SUCH AS:

- Bronchitis.
- Sore throat.
- Cold sores.
- Colds and flu (at the onset, as well as during).

- Toothache.
- Ear infection.
- Sinusitis.

*Acute conditions are short-lived, usually start quickly, and are relatively severe.
**Chronic conditions last for a long time, or recur frequently.

How to do the
Procedure for Acute Conditions:

1. Take four to six ounces of Noni fruit juice a day, as follows:
   - Sip two ounces of Noni fruit juice over the course of several minutes.
   - Several hours later sip one or two more ounces of Noni.
   - Sip another ounce or two several hours later.
2. Use topical and other internal Noni applications (as listed in Sections 2 and 3 of this book), to address each of your symptoms.

More about the Procedure
For Acute Conditions:

Continue to take four to six ounces of Noni a day until your symptoms go away. Afterwards, sip two or three ounces a day for about a week. Then return to a Maintenance Dose.

It may be more soothing to drink your doses hot. Try Noni Tea on page 115.

If you haven't found relief after three or four days, consult a health-care professional if you have not already done so.

16.

A PROCEDURE FOR CHRONIC CONDITIONS

Try this procedure for chronic conditions—those conditions which last for a long time, or recur frequently.

TRY THIS PROCEDURE FOR CONDITIONS SUCH AS:

- Aging.
- Allergies.
- Arthritis.
  (cont.)

- Asthma.
- Bronchitis.
- Broken bones.

- Degenerative diseases.
- Depression.
- Environmental Sensitivity.
- Fibromyalgia.
- Heart conditions.
- High cholesterol.

- Infections.
- Lupus.
- Neuralgia.
- Pain.
- PMS.
- Sinusitis.

How to do the
Procedure for Chronic Conditions:

1. For the first three days, take six ounces of Noni a day, preferably on an empty stomach. Take two of these ounces upon awakening, two in the afternoon, and the other two before bed.

2. Thereafter, take three ounces of Noni a day, preferably on an empty stomach. Take one of these ounces upon awakening, one in the afternoon, and the other before bed.

3. After your symptoms improve, Interrupt Noni Therapy for a few days. Then resume the three-ounce-a-day regimen.

If your chronic condition has a localized area, use the appropriate topical or internal Noni application as described in Sections 2 and 3 of this book.

More about the Procedure
For Chronic Conditions:

If the third dose, which is taken at bedtime, keeps you awake at night, take it earlier in the evening instead.

The Procedure for Chronic Conditions is designed to promote a slow and gradual improvement in overall health and well being. As a result, the underlying problem can be addressed—not just the symptoms.

Chronic conditions may take a while to improve, simply because you have had the condition for a long time and it may be deeply rooted in your body. As uncomfortable as your symptoms may be, your body has become accustomed to them.

As an added benefit to doing this Procedure, you may find relief from other conditions that you might have, especially discomforts such as: athlete's foot, cold sores, constipation, dandruff, gingivitis, indigestion, PMS, skin conditions, rashes, vaginal discharge, and yeast infection.

If your condition goes away completely, reduce your daily dosage to a Maintenance Dose. If your symptoms come back, return to the three ounces a day routine. After a few weeks, try Interrupting Noni Therapy (page 39).

If you consider your condition serious, debilitating, or life-threatening, consider doing a Procedure for Serious Conditions or the Procedure for Life-threatening Conditions.

17.

The Noni Chinese Body Clock Procedure

Taking Noni at specific times each day really can make a difference.

Try the Noni Chinese Clock Procedure when:

- Noni is no longer helping you as much as it once did.
- Your condition can be considered acute, chronic, or serious.
- You would like to get the most benefit from each dose of Noni that you take.
- You have the self-discipline to take Noni the same time each day, even if it means taking it in the middle of the night.

- Your body (or your budget) can handle only a small number of ounces of Noni each day, but your health condition warrants taking more.

- Your health condition involves organs listed on the chart on the following page.

How to do the
Noni Chinese Body Clock Procedure:

In this procedure, we want to take one ounce of Noni, two or three times a day, during the time periods that can best support the organs most responsible for our health.

1. Decide which two or three organs listed on the Chinese Body Clock chart are most responsible for your health condition. You may need to ask your health-care professional for his or her input on this question. Although it may seem that we have just one ailing organ, weaknesses in other organs usually exacerbate our primary condition.

2. Refer to the chart on the next page. Write down which time periods correspond to the organs you chose in Step 1.

3. Take a dose of Noni fruit juice during each of these time periods.

Here are some examples:

Let's say you have learned that a heart condition is complicated by a congested liver. Plan to take two doses of Noni: one at mid-day between 11:00AM and 1:00PM, and one in the very early morning between 1:00AM and 3:00AM.

Or you may have conditions that do not seem to relate to each other, such as a bladder infection and a bad cough. Take the Noni dose during the time periods that correspond to the ailing organs. In this case, the bladder and lungs. You might also take a dose between 9:00AM and 11:00AM, which corresponds to the immune system.

If your problem organs have adjacent time periods, such as the gall bladder (11:00PM - 1:00AM) and liver (1:00AM - 3:00AM), you could take your dose of Noni on the cusp between the two. In this case, at 1:00AM.

And, of course, if your condition is based on just one organ, with no other organs involved, take a dose of Noni during the time period that corresponds to that one organ.

THE CHINESE BODY CLOCK[15]

Organ	Time Period
Large Intestine	5:00AM - 7:00AM
Stomach	7:00AM - 9:00AM
Spleen	
(Pancreas, Immune System)	9:00AM - 11:00AM
Heart	11:00AM - 1:00PM
Small Intestine	1:00PM - 3:00PM
Bladder	3:00PM - 5:00PM
Kidney/Adrenals	5:00PM - 7:00PM
Pericardium	
(Circulation/Sex)	7:00PM - 9:00PM
Triple Warmer	9:00PM - 11:00PM
Gall Bladder	11:00PM - 1:00AM
Liver	1:00AM - 3:00AM
Lung	3:00AM - 5:00 AM

MORE ABOUT THE
NONI CHINESE BODY CLOCK PROCEDURE:

Years ago, the Chinese discovered that each major organ in the body was most active at a different time. Likewise, treating a weak organ during its corresponding time period was more beneficial than at any other time. The Noni Chinese Body Clock Procedure marries this knowledge with taking Noni. Those who try this procedure may find that their body needs less Noni, and that the Noni they do takes gives them better and more lasting results.

When you start this procedure, plan to reduce your doses of Noni. Let's say you usually take three ounces a day and have chosen two organs in Step 1. Reduce your daily intake of Noni to two ounces a day by taking one ounce during each of the time periods that correspond with the two organs. If you usually take two ounces a day and have chosen three organs, try taking one-half ounce during each of the three time periods. Do not cut your dose by more than one-half, especially if Noni is supporting a weakened condition. Pulling the support too quickly can imbalance your body's systems.

What if you discover that the organ you want to work on has a corresponding time period in the wee hours of the morning, when you are usually fast asleep? Your first thought may be, "no way am I going to wake up to take Noni at that time!" Consider this: is the sleep that you may lose worth the possibility of strengthening a problem organ? Why not try it for two or three days, to see how well it really works for you? Set your alarm or make an agreement with yourself to wake up (perhaps to go to the bathroom), during that time. Sometimes breaking a habit, routine, or mental concept (in this case about our sleep patterns), loosens our mindset enough to accept change, which can include healing.

In the end, if you find you are unable to take a dose of Noni in the middle of the night, the second best thing to do is to take a dose during the time period twelve hours away.

The "triple warmer system" on the Chinese Body Clock may be unfamiliar to you. The triple warmer regulates the body's fluids, temperature, and energy through respiration, digestion, and excretion.

It is possible to enhance this procedure and improve the effectiveness of Noni on a particular organ even more. To do this, take your dose of Noni at exactly the same time each day.

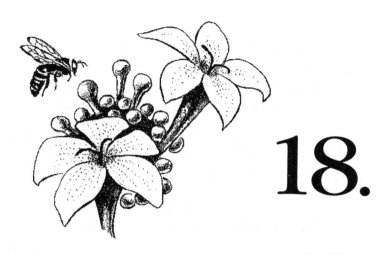

18.

A PROCEDURE FOR SERIOUS CONDITIONS 1

This procedure is designed for acute or chronic conditions that are considered "serious." Serious conditions disrupt a person's ability to lead a normal lifestyle. Serious conditions may not be immediately life-threatening, but have the potential to become so.

TRY THIS PROCEDURE FOR CONDITIONS SUCH AS:

- Addictions.
- Athletic injuries.

    (cont.)

- Cancer.

- Conditions that are very painful or debilitating.

- Plus any illness or disease that is commonly considered "serious," including infections and organ failure.

- Also, a nursing mother whose baby gets sick may use this procedure until her baby gets better. Noni's healing compounds pass through breastmilk to help the baby. Plus a mother may need the extra Noni to support herself through the stressful times of her child's illness.

HOW TO DO THE PROCEDURE FOR SERIOUS CONDITIONS:

1. Drink five to eight ounces of Noni fruit juice each day. Take one ounce upon awakening in the morning, and one before bed. Spread the other doses throughout the day.

2. If your condition has a localized area, refer to Sections 2 and 3 of this book to find topical or internal Noni applications that you can use on that area.

MORE ABOUT THE PROCEDURE FOR SERIOUS CONDITIONS:

For serious acute conditions, such as kidney or urinary tract infections and other infections, continue to follow this procedure for a week or so after your symptoms go away. Then gradually reduce your daily dose until returning to a Maintenance Dose.

For serious chronic conditions, you may have to follow this procedure for many months or more, even if you start to feel better. Every six weeks, try Interrupting Noni Therapy, unless it is not appropriate for your condition. Drinking this much Noni fruit juice may temporarily cause loose stools. Weigh this inconvenience against your body's present need for relatively large amounts of Noni. The stools will normalize once your body has completed its cleansing cycle and adjusted itself to this volume of Noni.

Sometimes, it can be a subjective decision as to whether your condition is serious enough to follow a Procedure for Serious Conditions, or if instead you should follow the Procedure for Chronic Conditions (page 57). If in doubt, start with a Procedure for Serious Conditions. After a few days, re-evaluate your condition. If you are feeling significantly better, gradually reduce the amount of Noni you are taking each day until you are following the Procedure for Chronic Conditions. But if your health starts to slip, return immediately to the higher dosage of Noni.

19.

A PROCEDURE FOR SERIOUS CONDITIONS 2

Here is another approach to taking Noni for serious conditions.

TRY THIS PROCEDURE FOR:

Any condition that you might consider "serious," including those on the list on pages 65 and 66.

And especially for:

- Auto-immune conditions.
- Nervous-system conditions.

(cont.)

- When the individual is very weak.
- If dehydration is present.

The Serious Conditions Procedure 2 may be Preferred over Procedure 1 when:

- You are using Noni for conditions of the extremities, such as the hands and feet.
- You have been using the Procedure for Serious Conditions 1 and would like to try something new.
- You have several different health conditions going on in your body.
- You typically drink less than eight glasses of water a day.
- Your condition has been difficult to diagnose.
- You would like a more economical approach to taking Noni for serious conditions. (This procedure uses less Noni than the Procedure for Serious Conditions 1.)
- The taste of Noni is repulsive to you.

How to do the Procedure for Serious Conditions 2:

1. Fill an eight to ten-ounce glass with purified water.
2. Measure one-half ounce (one tablespoonful) of Noni fruit juice.
3. Pour the Noni into the water. This is considered one dose.
4. Drink at least eight to ten of these doses per day, or more if you like. (This amounts to four to five ounces of Noni per day.)
5. Feel free to Sip (page 43) these doses or drink them All-at-Once (page 45).

More about the Procedure for Serious Conditions 2:

The first time you do this procedure, use a one-cup measuring cup to measure eight ounces of water. (One cup equals eight ounces.) Pour this into your drinking glass. This will let you know about how much water your drinking glass actually contains. Next time, simply fill your glass to about the same level or higher.

If you have a desire to drink other beverages while doing this procedure, feel free to do so. However, your first priority is to make sure that you drink your quota of at least eight doses of this Noni-water mixture per twenty-four hour period.

Use only distilled water, spring water, purified tap water, or clean-and-untreated well water for this procedure. Chlorine, fluorine, and other chemicals used to treat tap water will interfere with the body's ability to absorb and use Noni's healing compounds.

This procedure uses a total of four to five ounces of Noni fruit juice, as compared to the five to eight ounces suggested in the Noni Procedure for Serious Conditions 1. In Procedure 2, the body should utilize the Noni healing compounds more effectively because of the water. Water transports Noni's healing compounds to the areas of the body that need them, it helps the cells take in the compounds they need, and it also helps the body flush toxins and wastes.

Taking Noni in a glass of water lets you give your body Noni healing compounds more consistently throughout the day, especially if you sip the dose. This provides a kind of support that may be particularly effective with some conditions. In addition, taking Noni with water allows Noni's healing compounds to spread throughout the body more quickly than drinking undiluted Noni. This may be particularly helpful for conditions of the extremities, such as the hands and arms, legs and feet.

Here is another good reason to take Noni in water. Undiluted Noni can shock the body into a healing mode, whereas drinking Noni in water usually does not. In the case of severe illnesses, auto-immune conditions, and nervous system conditions; as well as in the presence of excessive fears, worry, and limiting mental concepts; the brain does its best to keep the body balanced. It may perceive undiluted Noni as a threat because Noni seems so strong and therefore the change it promises must also be strong. Although this change may be for the better, the brain may not think the body can handle it. As a result, the brain will initiate reactions to undiluted Noni, which may be thought of as cleansing or allergic reactions. But they are really the brain's way to tell a person not to initiate such strong changes so quickly. When Noni is added to a glass of water, its healing compounds are spread thinly throughout the water. As such, they are less likely to concern the brain's "gatekeeper," which is located on the tongue. These compounds are then free to uplift one's health without the brain's resistance.

A Procedure for Life-Threatening Conditions

Life-threatening conditions are defined as serious illnesses, diseases, or injuries that keep people bedridden and unable to, or nearly unable to, care for themselves. As with the other suggestions in this book, use this procedure in addition to protocols your doctor might recommend.

Use this Procedure for:

- Extensive injuries and burns.
- Serious conditions that are not responding to other forms of treatment.

(cont.)

- Serious illness or disease that has been getting worse for a long time.

- Times when the doctors say there is nothing else they can do.

How to do the Procedure For Life-threatening Conditions:

1. Drink one ounce of Noni fruit juice every hour. You may stretch the interval to every two hours during sleep time. Do this for three days. You may be taking as much as sixteen to twenty ounces of Noni a day.

2. Ask someone to apply a Noni Tummy Treatment (pages 237 and 243) on you. This may be especially helpful if you are physically unable to drink this much Noni.

3. After the first three days, drink one ounce of Noni every two hours. (Every three hours during sleep time.) Do this for about five days. You may be drinking as much as twelve ounces a day.

4. Then drink one ounce every three hours. Do this for three to six months. You will be drinking six to eight ounces a day.

5. Thereafter, continue to drink several ounces a day. At this point, try Interrupting Noni Therapy (page 39), for a few days every several weeks.

More about the Procedure For Life-threatening Conditions:

This procedure is designed to saturate the body with Noni fruit juice. This is accomplished more effectively if you spread your doses throughout the day. One or more doses may be taken as Noni Tea (page 115).

If you are physically unable to drink an entire ounce each time, reduce the doses to one tablespoonful. If waking up to take the dose is a problem, omit it, but take an extra ounce or two in the morning when you wake up.

If your condition has a localized area, refer to Sections 2 and 3 of this book to find topical or internal Noni applications that you can use there.

If your condition gets worse after you reduce your dosage as suggested in Steps 3, 4, and 5, return immediately to the higher dose. As you start feeling better again, reduce the amount of Noni you are taking more gradually than before.

Noni fruit juice can be taken with medications. However, Noni has been found to enhance their effect, so that less medication may be needed.[16] (If a physician has prescribed a particular dosage of medication for you, adjust this dosage only upon his or her recommendation.) Noni may also reduce the side effects of chemotherapy and radiation.

If you are too weak to drink or sip Noni, have someone give you drops of juice with an eyedropper, as often as every few minutes. If you feel nauseated taking Noni fruit juice, try adding some purified water to the Noni. Or, try taking the Noni in small sips, or with other juices or foods. But keep to the scheduled dose times. Do a Noni Tummy Treatment (pages 237 and 243), two or three times a day.

This procedure involves a considerable amount of Noni fruit juice. Be sure to have enough on hand so you won't run out. If taking this much Noni makes you feel better, but then your supply runs out, your progress may be seriously set back. Interrupting Noni Therapy (either intentionally or due to lack of Noni) is not suggested for seriously ill people until after they have felt considerably better for several months.

Sometimes, it can be a subjective decision as to whether your condition is "serious," and you should follow a Procedure for Serious Conditions, or "life-threatening" and you should follow the Procedure for Life-Threatening Conditions. If in doubt, start with the more intensive procedure. After a few days, reevaluate your condition. Cut back your daily dosage of Noni only if you are feeling significantly better. But if your health starts to slip, return immediately to the higher dosage.

Noni may not be able to help reverse a life-threatening condition. But concerned relatives can take heart in the fact that Noni may at least help to ease a loved one's suffering.

21.

A TECHNIQUE
FOR STUBBORN
CONDITIONS

This isn't "heavy artillery," but it may work like it. Varying your daily dose of Noni challenges your cells with change, which can stimulate them towards greater health.

TRY THIS TECHNIQUE WHEN:

- You've tried everything (including Noni) and a condition stubbornly won't get better.
- Certain symptoms improve, but then return.

(cont.)

- It seems you have reached a healing plateau, and can't seem to improve beyond it.
- Your condition is not considered "life-threatening" (see definition on page 73).

HOW TO DO THE TECHNIQUE
FOR STUBBORN CONDITIONS:

Use this technique after you have taken at least two ounces of Noni daily for two to three months, and still haven't achieved satisfactory results with a particular condition.

1. Calculate how many ounces of Noni you usually take each week. To do this, multiply the number of ounces of Noni you usually take each day, by seven days.

   For example, let's say you usually drink four ounces of Noni a day. Four times seven equals twenty-eight. Hence, you usually take a total of twenty-eight ounces of Noni a week.

   When doing this Technique for Stubborn Conditions, you will continue to take the same number of ounces of Noni per week, but vary the number of ounces that you take each day.

2. Plan ahead how many ounces of Noni you will take each day for the next four weeks. (See the examples on the following pages.) Write on a calendar the number of ounces you plan to take each day.

   Try to vary the doses as much as possible from day to day.

   - Schedule the same dose of Noni for no more than two days in a row.
   - If you usually take at least three ounces of Noni a day (twenty-one ounces per week), you could plan to take six to eight ounces or more of Noni one day a week.
   - Every two or three weeks, you could schedule a day in which you take zero ounces of Noni. This would give you some of the benefits of Interrupting Noni Therapy (page 39.)

3. Check your plan by adding up the number of ounces you've written down for each seven-day period. They should add up to the weekly amount you calculated in Step 1.

4. Every day, refer to your calendar to find out how many ounces of Noni you plan to take that day. Spread the doses throughout the day.

Note: The daily doses given in the following two examples are suggestions only. There are almost limitless scheduling possibilities.

EXAMPLE #1:

Step 1: Let's say you usually take two ounces of Noni a day. Multiply two times seven days per week, and you find that you usually take fourteen ounces of Noni a week.

Step 2: Your proposed weekly schedule could then be:

1 ounce on Monday

4 ounces on Tuesday

2 ounces on Wednesday

1 ounce on Thursday

3 ounces on Friday

1 ounce on Saturday

2 ounces on Sunday

14 ounces total

Step 3: In checking your plan, you find that these daily amounts total fourteen ounces. Good.

EXAMPLE #2:

Step 1: Let's say you usually take three ounces of Noni a day. Multiply three times seven days per week, and you find that you usually take twenty-one ounces of Noni a week.

Step 2: Your proposed weekly schedule could then be:

3 ounce on Monday

0 ounces on Tuesday

2 ounces on Wednesday

5 ounces on Thursday

1 ounce on Friday

8 ounces on Saturday

2 ounces on Sunday

21 ounces total

Step 3: In checking your plan, you find that these daily amounts total twenty-one ounces. Good.

More about the Technique For Stubborn Conditions:

Try this technique for a month. If it is helping, continue to take Noni in this way.

The Technique for Stubborn Conditions is based on the principle that our bodies and our cells will become complacent if they aren't challenged or stimulated. Complacent cells gradually become less healthy and vital. Change keeps our bodies alert. Alert cells, by nature, gradually grow healthier. Varying the doses of Noni that you take each day is one way to provide your cells with an environment of change. This can help challenge and stimulate your cells towards greater health.

22.

A Procedure to Gradually Introduce Noni to the Body

In some cases it is essential to introduce Noni very gradually to the body.

Use this Procedure for:

- Chemical poisoning.
- Heavy metal poisoning.

  (cont.)

81

- Hypersensitivity to supplements.
- Mercury poisoning.
- Parasites.
- Suspicion of allergy to Noni.
- Systemic yeast infections.
- Toxicity in the body.
- Weak or sensitive stomachs.
- Also, if a feeling of nausea occurs when you first try Noni.

How to Gradually
Introduce Noni to the Body:

This procedure begins with a topical Noni application.

1. Apply a Noni Tummy Treatment (page 237 and 243), daily for several days. This will help avoid a strong cleansing reaction that may occur if you start with oral doses.

   The bellybutton receives Noni's healing compounds better than skin elsewhere on the body. Hence, the Tummy Treatment is the next best thing to taking Noni orally.

   Proceed to Step 2 after your body can accept these daily treatments without showing signs of a cleansing reaction.

2. Try adding Noni fruit juice to your food for several days. (See pages 119-124 for recipes.) Consume no more than one tablespoonful of Noni in your food per day. You may continue with the daily Noni Tummy Treatments. Proceed to Step 3 after your body can handle Noni in foods without showing signs of a cleansing reaction.

3. When you are ready to try drinking Noni, you may discontinue both the Tummy Treatments and adding Noni to your food. Start with a small amount of 1:8 Dilution*, which is a special mixture of Noni and purified water.

   To make this mixture:

   a. Pour an ounce of Noni fruit juice into a jar.

*All fourteen Noni Dilutions and their unique effects are detailed in my book *Healing Secrets of Noni*.

b. Measure eight ounces of purified water in a measuring cup.

c. Pour the water into the jar in a slow, steady, uninterrupted stream. Meanwhile, swirl the jar for several seconds to mix the liquids together.

4. Measure one ounce of this Noni-water mixture, and pour it into a drinking cup. Seal the jar that contains the remaining mixture, and store it in the refrigerator. Several times a day, take a sip from the one ounce of the Noni-water mixture that is in the drinking cup.

5. Gradually increase the amount of this Noni-water mixture that you take each day. Your goal is to find an amount that allows you to detoxify and makes you feel better at the same time. Make more of the Noni-water mixture when your supply runs out.

MORE ABOUT THE PROCEDURE TO GRADUALLY INTRODUCE NONI TO THE BODY:

If drinking Noni makes you feel nauseated, it may be that your body is toxic (perhaps more than you may have thought). This procedure will help your body become accustomed to Noni, as well as help it to detoxify in a balanced way.

If you know the areas in your body where toxins have pooled, use a Noni Compress (page 143) over those areas.

If you have a buildup of mercury or other heavy metals in your mouth, try the Oral Detox Procedure (page 51) every day. Use a sip from the special Noni-water mixture described above to do the Oral Detox.

Noni Enemas (page 259) or a Noni Colonic Irrigation (page 262) may also be used to help the body become accustomed to Noni. In addition, these procedures will help flush toxins from your body.

The Noni Trauma Dose

Offer a Noni Trauma Dose as soon as possible after First Aid has been applied and you have attended to the individual's immediate needs.

Give Noni orally ONLY if the individual is awake, able to drink and not in shock.[17]

Use the Noni Trauma Dose for:

- Any sudden and traumatic experience.
- Back spasm.
- Broken bones.

    (cont.)

- Easing withdrawal symptoms from drugs, coffee, nicotine, and alcohol.(See Noni Quit-Smoking Techniques, page 89, and the Noni Technique for Alcohol Withdrawal, page 95.)
- Helping the body recover after surgery.
- Injuries and accidents.
- Preparing the body before surgery.
- Severe emotional trauma, such as profound grief, sadness, pain, or anger.

How to Take
A Trauma Dose:

A Trauma Dose consists of three or four ounces of Noni fruit juice taken All-at-Once. (Four ounces equals one-half cup.)

1. Measure three or four ounces of Noni fruit juice and pour it into a drinking cup. If possible Drink this All-at-Once (page 45). Drinking a Trauma Dose All-at-Once is a wake-up call that can send the body into a healing mode. Ideally, it will also counteract some of the effects of the trauma, thus reducing the trauma's negative impact on the body.

2. After giving the Trauma Dose, apply a topical application such as a Noni Compress (page 143), Noni Poultice (page 147) or Noni Tummy Treatment (pages 237 and 243), as appropriate for the condition.

3. Take a second Trauma Dose about six to ten hours after the first one.

4. Take a third Trauma Dose the next morning. Two or three Trauma Doses may be taken in a twenty-four hour period.

You may also take a tablespoonful of Noni fruit juice every hour or two. These doses may be sipped or taken as an Auto-dilution (page 47). Omit the doses during the sleeping hours, to allow yourself to rest without being disturbed.

Thereafter, take four to six ounces of Noni a day to support recovery. Take these doses one ounce at a time, spread throughout the day. These doses may be Sipped, taken All-at-Once or taken as an Auto-dilution. You may also take more Trauma Doses if needed.

MORE ABOUT
THE TRAUMA DOSE:

A Trauma Dose can help reduce pain, and help make you feel more calm, restful, and at ease. Tattered emotions may also be soothed. Healing and cell regeneration can be accelerated. Bleeding can be put under control.

If you are very weak and cannot drink the entire Trauma Dose, try to drink as much of it as possible.

When preparing for surgery, there will be a period of time beforehand during which you are asked not to eat or drink anything. Take your Noni Trauma dose just before this time period begins. After surgery, drink the Trauma dose as soon as you are able.

Some people might find it hard to drink so much cold Noni fruit juice All-at-Once if it is given straight from the refrigerator. You may not have time to warm the first Trauma Dose, but the following doses could be left at room temperature for a few hours.

24.

NONI
QUIT-SMOKING
TECHNIQUES

The information in this chapter first appeared in my book, *42 Ways to Use Noni Skin Lotion.* Since I wrote that book, I have received feedback from others and have had additional personal insights about addiction relief therapies using Noni. I would like to share this information again here, in an updated form, so that as many people as possible can benefit from it.

This chapter contains several Noni techniques that include Noni fruit juice, Noni skin lotion, Noni seed oil, and Noni liquid concentrate. If you practice all these techniques, both your physical and psychological need for cigarettes or other addictive substances should diminish. However, it is critical that you also want to be free of your addiction. Then, these techniques will offer more lasting results.

89

Use the Techniques
Described in this Chapter to:

- Quit smoking.
- Obtain relief from cravings during withdrawal.
- Alleviate withdrawal symptoms.

How to Use
Noni Quit-Smoking Techniques:

Here are several ways to use Noni, each of which plays an important role in helping to overcome addictions. These techniques will support your withdrawal both physically and psychologically. Begin them after you have taken your final dose of the addictive substance. You can either quit "cold turkey" or withdraw gradually. To withdraw gradually, try the Noni Fast Method 2 or the Noni Procedure for Serious Conditions 2. Each of these techniques includes a significant amount of both Noni and water. The Noni will help your body release its physiological need for cigarettes, while the water will help flush your body of nicotine.

Although these techniques can be used for any addiction, I have focused on how to quit smoking, since that is one of the most commonplace and destructive addictions that plague people today.

Drink daily doses of Noni fruit juice:

1. Drink one ounce of Noni fruit juice as soon as you wake up in the morning, before you eat or drink anything else but water. It may help to prepare that dose the night before, so it awaits you beside your bed when you awaken.

2. For the first three days after your last cigarette, drink another five ounces of Noni fruit juice each day, for a total of six ounces per day. Take each one-ounce dose two to three hours apart. Save one ounce to drink before bed.

3. Starting on the fourth day, drink a total of three ounces of Noni fruit juice daily. When you feel you are free of the addiction, reduce your dose to one or two ounces daily as maintenance.

Note:

Make sure you also drink at least eight to ten glasses daily of purified water, spring water, or distilled water.

The primary reason for drinking enough water and several ounces of Noni fruit juice when you quit smoking is to normalize your metabolism and flush your body of nicotine. Your body will need the extra Noni fruit juice during the first three days after your last cigarette, when the nicotine release is at its peak. Thereafter, three ounces a day should be enough until you are ready for a maintenance dose.

Don't be surprised if you or your family smells nicotine on your body, even though you are not smoking. This odor represents the nicotine that your body is eliminating through your skin.

TAKE NONI LIQUID CONCENTRATE ORALLY:

1. Put two drops of Noni liquid concentrate under your tongue, one on the right side and one on the left.
2. Do this every waking hour for three days. For the next week, do this three times a day. The following week you may need to do this only once a day.

Placing Noni liquid concentrate under your tongue allows Noni's healing compounds to go directly to your brain. Doing this every hour ensures that the brain is flooded with these compounds. This essential step helps your brain cells relearn how to prefer xeronine instead of nicotine. (This change of preference is explained under the heading "More about Using Noni to Quit Smoking," on page 93.)

The gradual reduction in dosages of Noni concentrate is meant to correspond with the decrease of nicotine in the brain.

Here are two techniques to use when cravings arise. Try each of the techniques to find out which works best. You may alternate these techniques one right after the other.

Noni seed oil Therapy:

1. Put one drop of Noni seed oil on a fingertip.

2. Rub this mixture above your upper lip and on the bottom of your nostrils. Focus on the aroma, if you are able to detect it (most smokers have a reduced sense of smell).

The mild aroma of Noni seed oil soothes and calms the brain, and helps take the edge off cravings. The midpoint between your nose and upper lip is also an energy point that, when stimulated by Noni seed oil, helps balance the left and right sides of the brain. This can help your cells adapt themselves to being nicotine free.

Ex-smokers can enjoy another benefit of this therapy: It allows your hand and arm to follow an ingrained pattern—that of moving towards your mouth. But rather than making this motion to bring a cigarette to your lips, you are bringing something healthy to them instead.

Noni liquid concentrate Therapy:

1. Put three drops of Noni skin lotion in the palm of your hand.

2. Add one drop of Noni liquid concentrate, and mix the ingredients together with a fingertip.

3. Put about half the mixture on one temple (the flat region on either side of your forehead), and half on the other.

4. Using your fingertips, rub both temples simultaneously, in a soothing circular motion. You may also rub some of the lotion onto your forehead. Your skin should soak up this mixture in about a minute.

This treatment serves two purposes. First, it is another way to get Noni's healing compounds into the brain—through the temples. Second, massaging the temples and forehead can alleviate the stress and tension that often occur when letting go an addiction.

Because this lotion-concentrate mixture is a brownish color that will be evident when applied to fair skin, some people may prefer to use Noni skin lotion by itself when at work or in public.

More about
Using Noni to Quit Smoking:

In addition to the Noni therapies listed in this chapter, drink extra water to help flush the nicotine from your system. The less nicotine in your body, the less you will crave it. Drinking at least eight to ten glasses of water a day is also essential to receive the maximum benefits of Noni's healing compounds. These compounds need water to work their best.

Now I'd like to take a moment and share why Noni works so well for addictions. This understanding is based on A. K. Olsen's interviews with Dr. Ralph Heinicke, the world's leading authority on xeronine. These interviews are recorded in the book, *Understanding the Miracle: An Introduction to the Science of Noni.*[18]

Xeronine is one of the many compounds that the body produces, which is essential for health. (Noni provides essential ingredients that the body needs to make xeronine.) Chemically, xeronine is a type of substance that is called an "alkaloid." Nicotine is also an alkaloid. In fact, the nicotine and xeronine alkaloids are shaped very much the same.

Other addictive substances, such as caffeine, cocaine, heroin, and morphine are also alkaloids that look very much like xeronine. However, the body does not get "addicted" to xeronine. And, one cannot get addicted to Noni.

The explanation in the following paragraphs refers to nicotine, but it pertains to these other alkaloids as well.

When an individual smokes a cigarette, the brain is flooded with nicotine. Because nicotine and xeronine look so much alike, the brain cells will accept nicotine in place of xeronine simply because there is more of it. If the brain is flooded with nicotine over several days, the cell receptors will actually adjust their shape so that they prefer the nicotine instead of xeronine. At this point, the individual is addicted. The brain cells now have a physical need for nicotine.

However, this action can also work in reverse. If you flood the brain with xeronine and stop providing additional nicotine, then

93

after several days the brain cell receptors will again adjust themselves. Only now they will prefer xeronine, as they normally
should, instead of nicotine.

Now there is no more addiction.

25.

A NONI TECHNIQUE FOR ALCOHOL WITHDRAWAL

This technique supports a gradual withdrawal from alcohol. To quit cold turkey, your body may need a great deal of additional support. You can receive this support by following the suggestions in the previous chapter, "Noni Quit-Smoking Techniques," which are meant for addictions of all kinds.

The Noni Technique for
Alcohol Withdrawal is for those who:

- Are not yet ready to stop drinking, but would like to alleviate some of the negative effects of alcohol on their body.
- Would like to withdraw gradually.
- Would like to try an approach that allows them to continue drinking, but naturally reduces their craving for alcohol.

How to do the
Noni Technique for Alcohol Withdrawal:

The technique is simple. Make an agreement with yourself that before you have any glass of wine, bottle of beer, shot of whiskey or any other alcoholic drink, that you first take one ounce of Noni fruit juice. That is the only rule: If you are going to drink an alcoholic beverage, first drink one ounce of Noni. No matter what. Do this before every alcoholic beverage you have. If you go out to drink, take a flask of Noni with you.

More About the
Noni Technique for Alcohol Withdrawal:

Taking an ounce of Noni before each alcoholic beverage may produce a number of different effects, or none at all. Your stomach may feel a little queasy, or you may get fully nauseated, which will naturally curb your drinking. Or you may get drunk more quickly, thereby decreasing your need for more alcohol. Or you may eventually get "turned off" by the alcohol and stop drinking. Over time, your desire for a drink should diminish. It may even go away after you take the ounce of Noni.

Noni's effect may be cumulative for some people. They may have to follow this procedure for a while before they suddenly experience Non's effects.

Another situation that may occur with this procedure is that the alcoholic will find the taste of Noni so repulsive that they refuse to drink it. Adding an ounce of Noni to one or two ounces of an alcoholic beverage can make the taste tolerable.

If you have a loved one who is an alcoholic, you may want to encourage them to do this procedure. However, alcoholics may feel threatened if you tell them the Noni will curb their desire for alcohol or help them stop drinking. Instead, tell them something else that is also completely true: tell them that taking an ounce of Noni before each beverage will help keep them healthy and alive. It will counteract some of the damage the alcohol is doing to their body. Assure them they don't have to quit drinking or drink any less. Then they may be more amenable to trying this technique. All an addict needs is to get enough Noni into their system, and their cells will begin to change. The cravings will eventually diminish in a natural, unstressful way.

Noni makes it easier to cut back the amount of alcohol that you drink, although quitting is most effective if you also summon your own desire and will-power.

After you have quit drinking, follow a Noni Procedure for Serious Conditions (pages 65 and 69) to help stabilize your body and ease withdrawal symptoms. As your body finds an addiction-free balance, gradually reduce the number of ounces of Noni that you take each day. Remember to drink an ounce of Noni whenever the desire for alcohol arises.

26.

NONI TECHNIQUE FOR FOOD ADDICTION RELIEF

Addiction to foods such as coffee, chocolate, or excessive sugar or carbohydrates is so commonplace that it has become a social norm. The degree of our addiction becomes apparent only when we try to make healthy changes to our diets.

TRY THE NONI TECHNIQUE FOR FOOD ADDICTION RELIEF WHEN:

- You are allergic to a particular food, but do not have the will-power to avoid it.

  (cont.)

- You are trying to lose weight by avoiding certain foods.

- You realize certain foods are harmful to your health, but are unable to remove them from your diet.

How to do the Noni
Technique for Food Addiction Relief:

1. Identify the food you would like to avoid. Select only one or two foods at a time.

2. Make an agreement with yourself that each time you reach for this food, that you will first drink a full eight- to ten-ounce glass of water to which you have added one-half to one ounce of Noni fruit juice. Then you are free to eat the food or not.

3. Optional: If you still feel a desire for the food, and sincerely want to avoid it, drink a second glass of the Noni-water mixture described in Step 3.

4. Eventually, after you drink your Noni-water mixture, your desire for this food will wane, and the choice to avoid it will become an easier one to make.

5. Make an agreement with yourself that you will follow this technique until you have gone at least fourteen days without eating the food(s) you chose in Step 1.

More about the Noni
Technique for Food Addiction Relief:

When choosing foods, be honest with yourself. If your problem is candy bars, for example, don't choose only one brand of candy bar to avoid…and then eat others. Choose all candy bars. If it is dairy, include all dairy products, etc.

When following this technique, omit the regular daily doses of Noni that you might usually take. On those days that you have no desire for the food chosen in Step 1—and therefore do not take the Noni-water mixture—be sure to drink one or two ounces of Noni as maintenance.

The first time you try this technique, use a measuring cup to measure eight ounces of water. Pour this amount into a drinking glass so that you have an idea how high to fill the glass next time without having to measure.

After drinking the Noni-water mixture and eating the chosen food, you may find yourself eating less of it than you would otherwise. This is partly due to the fact that your stomach is full of water. The Noni will also supply your body with certain nutrients, the lack of which may be causing your body to crave certain foods. Noni's healing compounds also modify cell receptor sites. These sites will eventually attract more healthful compounds, thereby reducing the body's physiological need for less healthful compounds. (To read about how Noni modifies receptor sites, see More About Using Noni to Quit Smoking, on page 93.)

The technique described in this chapter also works psychologically. It creates a span of time between a craving and the action of reaching for and eating the desired food. (During this time span, you are preparing a drink of Noni.) In the case of food addiction, this time span is usually characterized by a sense of "unconsciousness" or complete lack of control. Preparing a Noni-water mixture and drinking it before eating the desired food lengthens this time span. Do what you can to lengthen it enough that you can gain control over the situation and choose another food—or an activity other than eating.

While you are drinking the Noni-water mixture, you may be battling the strong pull to eat the chosen food. Keep your commitment to Noni. It may help to Sip (page 43) your Noni-water, drink it All-at-Once (page 45), or hold each sip in your mouth for several seconds before swallowing. It may also help to drink your Noni in a room other than the kitchen. Or go outside and drink it. Or telephone a friend. Ideally, do something healthful, or emotionally or mentally rewarding in order to take your mind off the craved food. Be creative, and experiment to see what works best for you.

The Noni Fast Method 1

What? Eat Only Noni?

Use the Noni Fast Method 1 if You:

- Are relatively healthy and would like to try a fast for general health maintenance.

- Want to experience a greater degree of health, well being and clarity.

- Suspect your body may harbor parasites and would like to use Noni to help get rid of them.

- Would like to use Noni to help clear yeast, infections, or viruses.

- Would like to adjust eating habits and correct bad ones.

How to Fast with Noni
Using Method 1:

1. During this fast, replace all the food in your diet and all the liquid that you would normally drink, with a special mixture of
   Noni and purified water. To make one dose of this mixture, which is also called a 1:8 Dilution:

   a. Pour one ounce of Noni fruit juice into a large drinking
      glass or one-quart jar.

   b. Measure eight ounces of purified water in a measuring
      cup.

   c. Pour the water into the Noni in a slow, steady, uninter-
      rupted stream. Meanwhile, swirl the glass for several sec-
      onds to mix the liquids together.

Note: One dose of this mixture equals nine ounces of liquid (one
ounce of Noni plus eight ounces of purified water).

2. Drink eight to ten (or more) of these Noni-water doses
   throughout the day. If you feel hungry, sip a dose or two.
   Continue the fast for seven days.

3. On the eighth day, start breaking the fast by eating foods that
   are easily digestible. Such foods include fresh fruit and cooked
   vegetables. Continue to drink the Noni-water doses as before.

4. On the ninth day, drink six to eight doses of the Noni-water
   mixture. Add a few more foods to your diet. Choose fruits,
   vegetables, whole grains, and protein sources that work for
   you. Avoid junk food and over-eating as your body is still
   recovering from the fast. Add two to four glasses of purified
   water to your diet.

5. On the tenth day, drink four to six doses of the Noni-water
   mixture. Broaden your diet slightly more.

6. On the eleventh day, drink two to four doses of the Noni-
   water mixture. Drink four to six glasses of purified water in
   addition to what you are now eating. Your diet should now
   be back to normal, and hopefully, you will have less desire for
   unhealthy foods.

7. On the twelfth day, the fast is over. Congratulations!

Resume your Noni Maintenance Dose. Be sure to drink at least eight glasses of purified water each day.

MORE ABOUT THE
NONI FAST METHOD 1:

You may fast for up to ten days if you are feeling well and are enjoying the effects of the fast. A less intense version of the Noni Fast Method 1 would be to do the fast (see Step 2) for three days instead of seven. Then follow Steps 3 through 7, which guide you through ending the fast slowly. Ending the Noni Fast slowly is important if you want your body to let go its cravings for certain foods, and therefore adjust your eating habits.

The Noni Fast is easier to do if you prepare several doses of the Noni-water mixture ahead of time. As you finish making each dose, pour it into a pitcher. Store the pitcher in the refrigerator.

Fasting helps the body clean out toxins and rebalance all body systems. A Noni Fast does the same and more. Noni has special properties that can enhance the immune system and help the body clear itself of yeast, fungus, parasites, bacteria, and viruses. Noni also helps the body's enzymes, cell receptor sites and other protein molecules work more effectively and efficiently. Hence, a Noni Fast does more than clean out toxins; it also helps to repair and rebuild the body.

Refer to Appendix B (page 305) to read about cleansing reactions. During this fast, you may experience cycles of both positive and negative cleansing reactions. The Noni Fast Method 1 can be intense. Consider doing the Noni Fast while you are on vacation from work, so you can get all the extra rest your body may need.

During the fast, consider using Noni Enemas (page 259) or a Noni Colonic Irrigation (page 261). These will help your body flush the toxins, parasites, and intestinal-wall build up that the Noni Fast is helping your body to release. Parasites may be expelled into the toilet.

When you are doing a Noni Fast, omit the daily dose of Noni that you might usually take.

Before you start a fast of any kind, consult a health-care professional who can let you know if fasting is safe for someone in your particular health condition.

28.

THE NONI FAST
METHOD 2

Here is another version of the Noni Fast.

USE THE NONI
FAST METHOD 2 IF YOU:

- Want the benefits of fasting, but don't want to stop eating or limit your diet in any way.

- Want the benefits of fasting, without having to change your lifestyle.

- Are not interested in initiating an uncomfortable cleansing reaction.

- Have health challenges, which don't permit you to stop eating.

107

How to Fast with Noni
Using Method 2:

1. During this fast, replace all the liquid in your diet (including water, coffee, tea, juice, soda pop, milk products, beer, and alcoholic beverages), with a special mixture of Noni and purified water.

   To make one dose of this special mixture, which is also called a 1:12 Dilution:

   a. Pour an ounce of Noni fruit juice into a quart-size jar.

   b. Use a two-cup measuring cup to measure twelve ounces (one-and-a-half cups), of purified water.

   c. Pour the water into the jar of Noni in a slow, steady, uninterrupted stream. Meanwhile, swirl the jar for several seconds to mix the liquids together.

   Note: One dose of this mixture consists of thirteen ounces of liquid (one ounce of Noni plus twelve ounces of purified water).

2. Drink six or more doses of this mixture each day. (Six doses is a little over nine-and-a-half cups of liquid.)

   Start with one dose before breakfast. Spread the other doses throughout the day, but take one whenever you are thirsty. These doses need not be taken on an empty stomach.

3. You may continue to eat during this fast. Focus your diet on fresh vegetables and fruits, whole grains, and protein foods that work for you. Avoid refined sugar, white flour, saturated fat, chocolate, food additives and preservatives, and processed foods.

More about the
Noni Fast Method 2:

Try this fast for three days at a time. Fasting any longer may initiate a cleansing reaction. If cleansing reactions do occur during the Fast, drink more of the Noni-water mixture to help your body flush the toxins that have been released. Also give yourself more rest and try deep breathing exercises. A Noni Enema (page 259) might also help.

The Noni Fast is easier to do if you prepare several doses of the Noni-water mixture ahead of time. As you finish making each dose, pour it into a pitcher and store the pitcher in the refrigerator.

People often loose weight while fasting. Since foods are not limited with this fast, however, weight loss may or may not occur. If you would like to lose weight, try sipping a dose of the Noni-water mixture when you feel hungry. This may reduce your appetite.

When you are doing a Noni Fast, omit the daily dose of Noni that you might otherwise be taking.

THE NONI
FAST METHOD 3

For those of us who want to release toxins, but don't like to give up eating.

USE THE NONI FAST METHOD 3 IF YOU:

- Are relatively healthy and would like to initiate a cleansing reaction.

- Would like the benefits of fasting without having to cut out food.

- Would like to carefully control the detoxification process.

How to Fast with Noni
Using Method 3:

To do this fast, you will be taking a dose of Noni at precisely regular intervals for a certain number of hours each day, for a certain number of days. For example, you might take one teaspoonful of Noni every thirty minutes between noon and 5:00PM for three days.

1. Read about the Four Variables of the Noni Fast 3 in the box on the next page. Select a Noni Dose you would like to take, a time interval, a time duration, and a number of days. During the fast, you will be able to modify these selections depending on how you feel. Use the spaces provided to write down your initial choices:

   How much Noni per dose? _____
   What time interval? _____
   How many hours per day? _____
   How many days? _____

2. After you have chosen from the Four Variables, find out how much Noni you will need each day:

   A. Count how many doses you plan to take per hour. Multiply this number times the number of hours you plan to do this fast per day.

   B. Multiply your answer in Step 2A times the dose amount you chose in Step 1. This will tell you how much Noni you are planning to take each day. If this amount seems like too much, go back to Step 1 and reduce the dose amount you initially chose.

3. Before you begin the fast, make sure you have enough Noni available. To find out the total amount of Noni you will need, multiply the answer you got in Step 2B times the number of days you plan to do the fast. Use the Table on page 5 to convert teaspoonfuls and tablespoonfuls to ounces.

4. When you are ready to begin, take your first dose and

mark what time it is.

5. Set a clock timer to alert you when to take your next dose. Or, use an oven timer.

6. When the timer rings, take your next dose. Repeat Steps 4, 5 and 6 for as many hours as you have chosen in Step 1.

THE FOUR VARIABLES OF THE NONI FAST 3:

1. The Noni Dose :

This can be as small as a sip or as much as a tablespoonful of Noni. The larger the dose, the more powerful the fast will be.

2. The time interval :

This can be as frequent as five minutes or as long as one hour. The more frequent the interval, the more attention you will have to give to this fast, and the more intense it will be.

3. The time duration per day :

This can be as short as one hour or as long as about twelve hours. However, it must be long enough that you are able to take at least five doses. Select a duration that you can commit to each day for the number of days that you want to do this fast. During the fast, you may opt to cut back the duration based on how you feel.

4. The number of days you would like to continue this fast :
This can be one day or as many as about fourteen. As the fast progresses you may choose to modify the number of days you have chosen.

More About the
Noni Fast Method 3:

Do not underestimate the power of this fast. It can bring on an intense cleansing reaction. Please refer to page 305 for a list of possible reactions. In addition, you may feel a sense of increasing intensity with every dose you take, especially after a few doses when your body realizes the rhythm you have initiated.

This fast is powerful because of the rhythm of taking Noni at pre-defined intervals. A healthy body is accustomed to regularity of all its functions and cycles. As our health declines, our rhythms and cycles start to break down. They weaken and become less reliable. This Fast forces the body into rhythm—an effect that is enhanced by regularly presenting it with something healthful like Noni fruit juice.

The body responds very quickly to this forced rhythm. It uses the rhythm you set up like a template, which encourages other rhythms in our body to tighten up and become more regular. Interestingly, it does not seem to matter what kind of rhythm we establish for this Fast, the effect on the body will be the same. I suspect that we will design the Fast in a way that not only suits our schedule and our ability to follow, but whatever we design will also be the perfect template for our body's systems.

The first thing that usually happens when the body's rhythms are tightened is that the cells initiate a cleansing. This Fast allows you to control how quickly this cleansing occurs. To alleviate cleansing reactions, take less Noni per dose, increase the time interval between doses, and/or cut down the number of hours per day that you do the Fast. Conversely, to intensify the fast, take more Noni per dose, shorten the time interval between doses, and/or lengthen the number of hours per day that you do the Fast.

30.

NONI TEA

Adding hot water to Noni will not hurt the healing compounds in the juice. On the contrary, I believe the body absorbs Noni's healing compounds more readily when the Noni is taken at room temperature or warmer.

USE NONI TEA:

- At the onset of flu-like symptoms.
- As a tonic before or during flu season.
- As a tonic before or during times of unusual stress.
- For immune deficiency conditions, in place of regular doses of Noni.
- For throat conditions including sore throat, swollen glands, and tonsillitis.
- To help relieve the symptoms of colds and flu.
- To help you relax after a stressful day.

115

How to Make Noni Tea:

1. Pour one ounce of Noni fruit juice into a teacup or mug. (Don't use plastic or paper cups.)

2. Boil about a cup of purified water. (Use a glass, enamel or stainless steel pot.)

3. Pour exactly five ounces of the hot water into a glass measuring cup. Hold the cup at eye-level to make sure the measurement is accurate.

4. Pour the five ounces of hot water into the teacup in a slow, steady, uninterrupted stream. Meanwhile, stir the liquids, or swirl the cup, to mix the Noni and water together.

5. Sip, as you would drink tea.

More about Noni Tea:

One dose of Noni Tea consists of five ounces of hot purified water added to one ounce of Noni fruit juice.

To double the dose, add ten ounces of hot purified water to two ounces of Noni fruit juice. You will need an extra-large mug for this. Double doses of Noni Tea are especially helpful at the onset of flu-like symptoms. They may also be used for the Procedure for Acute Conditions, on page 55.

To make Noni Tea, you may use spring water, distilled water, filtered water, or pure well water. Do not use chlorinated or fluoridated water. These chemicals may interfere with the body's ability to absorb Noni's healing compounds.

Hot Noni Tea feels wonderfully soothing on a sore throat. But if your Noni Tea cools off, it is still beneficial to drink.

Check the temperature of Noni Tea before giving it to children, to make sure it isn't too hot for them.

For colds and flu, drink Noni Tea three to five times a day. See also Noni Ear Drops (page 253) and Noni Nose Drops (page 273). For bronchial conditions and coughing, try a Noni Poultice (page 147) over the lungs.

31.

THE NONI TONIC

The Noni Tonic consists of taking Noni Tea in place of one's usual Noni doses to help boost the immune system, and help the body handle stressful situations.

TAKE A NONI TONIC BEFORE POTENTIALLY STRESSFUL SITUATIONS SUCH AS:

- Birthdays, holidays, or anytime you plan to eat greater quantities of food, or more sugar, fat, and refined foods than usual.
- Events which may be particularly stressful, such as exams, presentations, speeches, and competitions.
- Surgery.
- The beginning of school (or day care for young children).
- Traveling, especially out of the country.

How to Take
A Noni Tonic:

1. Before the anticipated event, drink a dose of Noni Tea three or four times a day, preferably on an empty stomach. To make Noni Tea, see page 116.

   • Start a few days before one-day events such as birthdays and presentations.

   • Start two weeks before extended events, such as school or traveling, or particularly stressful events such as surgery.

2. If possible, continue to take the Noni Tonic the day of the event. If the event lasts more than a day, continue to take the Noni Tonic until the event ends. Then return to your usual Noni dosage.

More about
The Noni Tonic:

Teenagers can take the same dosages and amounts as adults. Give older children two doses of Noni Tonic (in the form of Noni Tea) daily. Make one dose of Noni Tea for young children, and give them half of this dose twice a day.

If your children refuse to drink Noni Tea, try giving them Noni in other ways. See page 126, for a list of creative ways to give Noni to children.

If you are following the Procedure for Acute Conditions or for Chronic Conditions, you may substitute each ounce of Noni that you would usually take, with one dose of Noni Tea. Similarly, if you are following the Procedure for Serious Conditions and would like to take the Noni Tonic to help prepare for surgery, simply replace all of your usual Noni doses with doses of Noni Tea. For example, if you usually drink one ounce of Noni fruit juice three times a day, instead take one dose of Noni Tea three times a day. (Remember, one dose of Noni Tea equals five ounces of purified water added to one ounce of Noni fruit juice.)

32.

Noni in Foods

To obtain the full benefit from Noni's healing compounds, it is best to take Noni on an empty stomach. But sometimes this can be too much to ask of children or other family members who may object to Noni's taste—or even to the idea of taking supplements.

An option is to include Noni in Foods. Eating Noni with foods may destroy some of Noni's healing compounds in the stomach's digestive juices. But other compounds must still work, as Noni is an effective Anti-acid Substitute (page 249) when taken after meals.

Include Noni in Foods When:

- Adding Noni fruit juice to foods may be the only way a child will take Noni orally.
- You feel nauseated when you try to drink Noni.
- You want the benefits of Noni, but don't care for the taste.
- You have a sensitive stomach or a toxicity condition.
- You want to add Noni to your family's meals as a tasty, and healthful ingredient.

119

HERE ARE SOME IDEAS FOR
ADDING NONI FRUIT JUICE TO FOODS:

SAUCES AND SPREADS:

- Mix one ounce of Noni fruit juice with one-quarter to one-half cup of blueberry sauce. Pour this on cheesecake, pancakes or waffles.

- Beat together two to three ounces of Noni fruit juice with a half cup of softened butter. The butter will turn lavender-pink. Store in the refrigerator. Spread on breads and muffins.

- Add one tablespoonful of Noni fruit juice to the jelly jar and mix. Try this for making peanut butter and jelly sandwiches.

- Mix one ounce of Noni fruit juice with one ounce of tahini or peanut butter. Mix in two to four teaspoonfuls of soy sauce to taste. Use as a sauce over vegetables and grains.

- Combine equal parts of Noni fruit juice, peanut butter, and maple syrup to cover almost anything.

- Beat eight ounces of softened cream cheese with one ounce of Noni for a lightly colored lavender spread. Add two ounces for a slightly darker color and a softer spread. Use on crackers and sprinkle with dried dill weed.

SOUPS:

- Add one, two, or three teaspoonfuls of Noni fruit juice per serving of canned or homemade soup after cooking.

SALADS AND DRESSINGS:

- Add an ounce or two of Noni to any commercial salad dressing bottle. Shake well before serving.

- Add a teaspoon or more of Noni per serving of fruit salad.

- Mix shredded carrots with raisins, coconut, honey, cinnamon, and Noni fruit juice. Add one or two tablespoonfuls of Noni per cup of shredded carrots.

- Try "Tahitian Tuna Salad" using tuna, mayonnaise, chopped carrots and celery, coconut, pineapple, and Noni fruit juice. Add one tablespoonful of Noni per cup of tuna salad.

- Make "Noni Compoti" with canned pear halves that are filled with a teaspoonful of Noni fruit juice then a dollop of cottage cheese. Top with a maraschino cherry.

GRAINS:

- After cooking white rice, add an ounce or two of Noni fruit juice. Use a fork to fluff the rice and mix in the juice. The Noni will give the rice a light purple color.

- Noni fruit juice may also be added to cooked whole grains. Add sesame seeds and raisins to emphasize the fruity flavor.

- Make "Rigatoni Noni" using cooked rigatoni noodles. Add Noni fruit juice to heated tomato sauce. Mix with the noodles. Top with grated Parmesan cheese.

    Adding Noni to tomato sauce is a foolproof way to "hide" Noni's flavor. Try adding a tablespoonful or more per serving—and your family may never know it's there.

VEGETABLES:

- Mash sweet potatoes, then add butter, honey, cinnamon, and a teaspoonful or two of Noni fruit juice per serving.

- Add Noni fruit juice to cooked carrots, green beans and onions after they've been cooked. Use a teaspoonful or two of Noni per serving.

- Sauté leafy greens and mushrooms. When done cooking, add a teaspoonful of Noni fruit juice per serving.

MEAT/FISH/POULTRY/TOFU/TEMPEH MARINADES AND SAUCES:

Cooking foods that have been marinated in Noni may destroy

some of Noni's healing compounds. So use Noni in marinades for flavor, and for its tenderizing effect on meats and poultry.

- Try a marinade made with one ounce of Noni fruit juice, two ounces of orange juice concentrate, two teaspoonfuls of soy sauce (or more to taste), one ounce of berry juice (raspberry, cherry, or blueberry), and two ounces of finely chopped red onion. Garnish the cooked dish with fresh berries in season.

- Try one or two tablespoonfuls of Noni in your favorite marinade recipe.

- Dip cooked shrimp in a mixture of one ounce of horse-radish, one ounce of ketchup, and a tablespoonful of Noni fruit juice. The Noni significantly reduces the sharpness of the horseradish.

- Try a sauce made from two or three cloves of crushed garlic, one ounce of Noni fruit juice and one ounce of soy sauce. Wow!

- Add a tablespoonful of Noni fruit juice per quarter-cup to half-cup of barbecue sauce.

- Sprinkle one tablespoonful of Noni fruit juice over each cup of stuffing, after it has been cooked and removed from the turkey.

DESSERTS:

- Mix equal parts of Noni fruit juice and chocolate or straw-berry sauce for an ice cream topping.

- Make homemade ice cream flavored with Noni and other fruits and berries. Or simply use these as a topping for store-bought ice cream or frozen yogurt.

- Add fruit chunks, honey, and a teaspoonful or two of Noni fruit juice to plain, unsweetened yogurt. Sprinkle with nuts or wheat germ.

- Add one tablespoonful of Noni to spiced apple cider.

- Sprinkle one to three ounces of Noni fruit juice on top of fruit pies, cobblers and bread pudding after cooking.

- Make butter-cream frosting using butter and confectioner's sugar. Use Noni instead of water or milk. The Noni will color the frosting a pretty lavender-pink.

- Make a fruity Noni gelatin dessert by dissolving one package of unflavored gelatin in two cups of a natural fruit juice. Heat while stirring until the gelatin is dissolved. Pour the hot liquid into serving bowls.

  Add chopped bananas, grapes, apples or other favorite fruit. Then add one teaspoonful of Noni fruit juice per serving. Put the gelatin in the refrigerator to set.

  If you pour Noni into a light-colored fruit juice and stir, the fruit juice will become a darker color throughout. If you pour the Noni in very gently and don't stir, the Noni pulp will form a pretty "cloud" which settles at the bottom of the bowl.

MORE ABOUT NONI IN FOODS:

The therapeutic effects of Noni added to foods may be less immediate, and not as strong as Noni fruit juice taken by itself on an empty stomach.

The amounts of Noni given in the recipes on the previous pages are suggestions only. Adjust the amount to suit your taste and preference.

How much Noni you can add to a recipe depends on how well the juice combines with the other ingredients and how important it is to mask the Noni's flavor. Generally, recipes can incorporate a teaspoonful to a tablespoonful of Noni per serving.

Add Noni to foods after they have been cooked. This will preserve the heat sensitive compounds in Noni.

Noni fruit juice has been pasteurized during processing. However, the heating temperature used is carefully regulated so that Noni's healing compounds remain intact. In fact, most of these compounds are unaffected by these temperatures. However, cooking can easily raise the temperature beyond the acceptable limits, thereby hurting the more heat sensitive compounds.

Noni affects various foods in different ways. For example, Noni fruit juice lends an attractive light purple color to some white and light colored foods, such as white rice and potatoes. It can give other foods a brownish tinge. Noni enhances the flavor of some foods, such as garlic, and subdues the flavor of others, such as horseradish. Some foods, like tomato sauce, mask Noni's flavor.

If you aren't accustomed to eating sugar, then Noni might help you handle its effects. Either add the Noni to the dessert recipe, or drink it after eating the sugary food. Of course, this does not give license to diabetics or other sugar-sensitive people to eat foods they should otherwise avoid. But this tip can be helpful at birthdays and other holiday occasions.

When you are making a large recipe with many servings, you may want to know how much Noni you should add. Multiply the amount of Noni you would like each person to receive by the number of servings in your recipe. This will give you the total amount to add.

33.

GIVING NONI
TO CHILDREN

"You want me to drink, What?"

BABIES AND YOUNG CHILDREN:

Healthy babies, toddlers, and children up to the age of about eight or nine probably don't need to drink Noni fruit juice every day. They might even resist the juice when you try to give it to them. If they are healthy, trust their body's innate intelligence. Offer them Noni every day when you drink yours, to accustom them to a routine and to a lifestyle that includes Noni fruit juice. If they refuse to drink any, at least let them see that you take Noni daily.

At times, you may want to insist your children take Noni. For example as a tonic to support their immune system before a vacation, before the holidays, before school begins, or after they have eaten something very sweet like a helping of birthday cake. Some creative ways to make Noni more appealing to children are listed below. (See also The Noni Tonic on page 117.)

Youngsters who become ill or injured will have a specific need for Noni, and tend to take it readily and eagerly. In this case, give them as much Noni fruit juice as they will drink—within reason. Use topical applications freely. One dose may be all they need to alleviate relatively mild conditions.

Seriously ill children can follow the Procedures for Serious Conditions (page 65 and 69) or for Life-Threatening Conditions (page 73). Give babies and toddlers one-quarter of each dose suggested for adults. Older children can take one-half of each of the doses. But give more if they are willing and eager to drink it.

Drinking Noni fruit juice may soften a child's stools. But this can be helpful if a child is taking antibiotics, which often cause constipation. You will have to weigh the temporary inconvenience of loose stools with the tremendous benefits the child will receive from taking Noni.

Here are Two Secrets for Successfully Giving Noni to children:

1. Make it fun.
2. Don't make a fuss over it.

Creative Ways to Give Noni To Babies and Children

- Mix Noni with another fruit juice. Or, make a version of Noni Tea using five ounces of apple or grape juice and one ounce of Noni. Some children may prefer this mixture warmed.

- Make homemade frozen juice-pops with Noni fruit juice mixed with other fruit juices.

- Mix Noni with applesauce, cottage cheese, or other favorite foods.

- Give Noni to infants with an eyedropper, or add it to their bottles.

- Try giving Noni to children while they take a bath. This can be fun, and if any Noni is spilled, their clothes won't get stained.

- Let children drink their Noni with a straw.

- Give children their Noni in a colorful container that is usually not used for drinking, such as a toy stacking-cup.

- Let them choose a special cup from your cupboard, or buy a special one at the store that will be used only for drinking Noni.

- Let them drink straight from the Noni bottle. Though you won't know exactly how much they drink, their body's intelligence will likely inspire them to take as much as they need.

- Play a pretend game with your child. Build a bird's nest with sheets and towels. Pretend your child is a baby bird and you are the father or mother bird. What do baby birds eat? Worms, of course! Pretend you are giving your baby bird a worm, using an eyedropper filled with Noni fruit juice. Worms taste yucky, but baby birds love them. Show your child how baby birds tilt their heads back and open their mouths for their parents to put in food. After a baby bird eats a worm, she ruffles her little wings and opens her mouth for more (ruffling her "wings" may distract your child from the Noni's taste).

- Try appealing to reason. Point out all their symptoms, and explain how Noni might help. Explain that Noni fruit juice can help their bodies fight germs. It can help them be strong and healthy so they can go out and play again sooner.

- Get on your hands and knees and beg. (Just kidding!)

- If a child flat-out refuses to drink Noni fruit juice, you might apply a Noni Tummy Treatment instead. If necessary, this may be done at night while the child is sleeping. It can also be applied each time a baby is diapered.

- Let drinking Noni fruit juice become a natural part of your family's daily routine. Use Noni topical and internal applications often. Let Noni be one of the first things that come to mind when you think about using a home remedy.

PRE-TEENS AND TEENS:

When children enter the pre-teen and teen years, they could benefit from a daily dose of Noni fruit juice. It may help ease the many transitions their bodies are making.

If teens aren't forced to drink Noni, they will be more willing to take it. Still, they may watch what Noni does for their parents first before they try it themselves. Let them know the juice is available for them.

Tell them that Noni can be used both orally and topically to help some conditions that are of particular concern to teens. For example, Noni can help clear the skin, stabilize mood swings, ease growing pains, enhance athletic performance, and speed recovery time for athletic injuries.

Teens may follow the same procedures and take the same doses as adults. Teens who weigh less than one hundred pounds may take half the suggested amounts.

KEEPING NONI A
FAMILY FRIEND

Here are some ways to keep Noni a family friend, even after the initial excitement of using Noni wears off.

THE IDEAS IN THIS
CHAPTER CAN BE HELPFUL FOR:

- All members of the family.
- General health maintenance.
- The long-time Noni enthusiast.

How to Keep
Noni a Family Friend:

Here are some ideas for incorporating Noni into a family lifestyle:

- Make a ritual of giving everyone in the family their daily dose of Noni at the same time and place.

- When injuries occur, remember Noni. Refer to the chapter on Noni First Aid (page 189).

- Let your children observe how you reach for Noni after minor cuts and burns, and other injuries.

- Become familiar with the topical and internal Noni procedures described in this book. Experiment with them, and find out which ones work best for you. When a situation arises that may be helped by one of these procedures, you will be more comfortable using it if you have already experimented with it beforehand.

- Let your children help you make and apply various topical applications including Noni Paste, Noni Poultices, and Noni Compresses.

- Make it a habit to turn to Noni whenever a health condition arises.

- At the first sign of colds or flu, make it a habit to take extra doses of Noni or make Noni Tea (page 115).

- Always have Noni fruit juice available, and never run out.

- Keep at least two extra bottles of Noni available for emergencies, when extra doses may be required.

- THINK Noni. Whenever a health condition arises, THINK Noni. Make this your motto.

- When Noni doesn't seem to be working as before, keep the faith, be creative, and try a new way to use Noni.

- Keep this book handy for reference.

MORE ABOUT
KEEPING NONI A FAMILY FRIEND:

Noni is here to help you and your family. It is Nature's Gift. All you have to do is be willing to try it, use it, and keep looking for new ways that it can help you. It is important to be creative and flexible with Noni, and be ever willing to experiment and try new ways to work with it. The ideas in this book give you an excellent start.

35.

GIVING NONI TO CATS AND DOGS

The following tips for giving Noni fruit juice to cats and dogs are not meant to replace your veterinarian's advice. Use them in addition to the therapies your vet suggests.

HOW TO GIVE
NONI TO CATS:

Some cats don't mind you injecting Noni fruit juice into their mouth. Others won't stand for it. Here is another way to give these felines their Noni.

1. Fill a clean plastic syringe with a dose of Noni fruit juice.

2. Optional: Hold the syringe in a bowl or sink full of hot water to warm the juice. Most cats probably don't care

whether or not you warm their Noni. Those who are very ill, might appreciate it.

3. While petting your cat with one hand, hold the syringe with the other hand. Slowly apply the juice to the cat's side, near the base of her tail, or on her hind leg. These areas should be relatively easy for the cat to reach.

   Massage the juice into her fur so it doesn't drip off her body.

4. The cat will lick off the juice, thereby ingesting it.

More about Giving Noni to Cats:

Injecting Noni into a cat's mouth may be necessary if the cat is too old or ill to thoroughly lick off the juice.

If your cat has long hair, consider brushing her before you apply the Noni. This way, she will be less likely to ingest excessive hair when she washes off the Noni.

Key to giving Noni to cats (and dogs) is using a plastic syringe tube. You can find them in pet stores. They are typically used to hand feed small animals and baby parrots.

Here are some guidelines for how much Noni to give your cat, and how often.

- For injuries, apply the juice directly on the wound. Also give the cat one tablespoonful of Noni two times a day. Apply it to her fur or inject it directly into her mouth.

- For chronic conditions, give your cat one or two teaspoonfuls of Noni, two or three times a day.

- For serious or life-threatening conditions, try giving two teaspoonfuls, four to eight times a day. You may have to apply the juice directly in the cat's mouth with an eyedropper or plastic syringe.

- For trauma, and both before and after surgery, give a one-ounce dose. This will help speed recovery. During recovery, you can also give one teaspoonful every few hours.

- Continue Noni therapy until the condition improves, then reduce or discontinue the dose.

- A single one-ounce dose can sometimes be all that is needed for relatively minor health conditions.

- A feline Maintenance Dose would be about one teaspoonful a day.

Dosages for animals are usually measured in CCs. Your plastic syringe tube may therefore list only CCs. Here are the equivalents:

One teaspoonful = 5 CCs.

One tablespoonful = 15 CCs.

One ounce = 30 CCs.

HOW TO GIVE
NONI TO DOGS:

Before trying creative ways to give Noni fruit juice to your dog, see if he will drink it by himself. (It doesn't hurt to try.) Offer him some in a bowl either alone or mixed with an amount of water that he will drink at one time. If that doesn't work:

1. Fill a large plastic syringe tube with Noni fruit juice.

2. Have your dog sit.

3. Position yourself beside his right shoulder. Stand or kneel, depending on your dog's size. Hold the syringe in your right hand. Show him the syringe and let him sniff it. Give him lots of pats and praise.

4. Wrap your left arm around your dog and slide your left hand under his chin. Gently lift his chin so that he is looking up. He may respond by kissing you.

5. Insert the end of the syringe tube inside the back corner of his lips. This can be done on either the right or left side of his face (whichever side works best for you). The end

of the syringe should be pointing down, between the inside of his cheek and his teeth. Your left hand should be underneath his lower jaw, gently keeping his chin pointed towards the ceiling. You don't need to open his mouth or insert the syringe between his teeth.

6. Squeeze the juice between his lips as fast as he will drink it. He will use his tongue to lap it up. The trick is to keep his nose pointing up, and the syringe pointing down. Reassure him by talking to him constantly, and looking kindly in his eyes.

Have patience, and always praise. Sooner or later, you'll be able to give him Noni fruit juice without spilling a drop! (Well, maybe just one or two.)

More about Giving Noni to Dogs:

Try the Noni oral, topical and internal applications listed in this book that are appropriate for your dog's condition. You may need to modify the procedures to suit him, and some of course, just won't work for pets. (Can you imagine your dog doing the Noni Gargle!)

Dogs that weigh over one hundred pounds can receive the same doses, according to the same procedures, as adult humans. Give medium-size dogs the same amount as you would give children, and small dogs the same amount as you would give to cats.

You can find large plastic syringe tubes, which can hold up to two ounces of liquid, in pet stores that specialize in parrots. These large syringe tubes are used to hand feed baby macaws.

36.

GIVING NONI
TO HORSES

For horses and ponies, from backyard pets to racehorses.

WHEN TO GIVE NONI TO HORSES:

- To enhance performance.
- To improve health and overall condition.
- To prepare for show and racing.
- To enhance recovery from illness, disease, and injury.

HOW TO GIVE NONI TO HORSES:

Noni can be given to horses both orally and topically.

- When giving Noni orally, it is best to give it without food, which is also true for humans. Fill a syringe with the amount of Noni you wish to give. Insert the syringe into the corner of the horse's mouth as if you were administering paste wormer, and squirt the Noni in.

- Some horses associate the syringe with the unpleasant experience of being wormed, and will refuse to take Noni this way. The second best method is to offer Noni in a small bowl. However, if the horse smacks her lips and tongue while savoring the taste of Noni, she can send drops of Noni flying in all directions. This can be messy and wasteful.

- If your horse cannot drink Noni politely from a bowl, you will have to add the Noni to his grain rations.

1 ounce = 2 Tablespoonfuls = 30cc = 30ml
2 ounces = 4 Tablespoonfuls = 60cc = 60ml

How Much Noni to Give Horses:

If your horse is healthy, start with one or two ounces of Noni daily. After a week—if you began with one ounce—increase the dose to two ounces a day as maintenance. You will know that your horse is getting too much Noni when his stools get too loose, or his energy and zest for life become more than you can handle. Then reduce the daily dose to one ounce. You might even have to eliminate Noni from his diet for a while.

When treating illness or injury, start with a two-ounce dose. Administer a second two-ounce dose several hours later. Observe your horse's behavior carefully and adjust the amount of Noni accordingly. For example, if she is feeling better, continue giving her two, two-ounce doses of Noni daily until her stools loosen or she becomes too zesty. If she is injured and needs to rest—but the Noni is making her too lively—reduce the oral doses. You can also focus on topical applications. If her condition does not seem to be improving, give her a third two-ounce dose. And if necessary after a few days of non-improvement, you might even try a fourth.

Here are some ideas
For applying Noni topically:

- Mix equal parts of Noni fruit juice and Noni skin lotion. Massage into the area. This can be especially helpful for tight, stiff, or overworked muscles.

- Mix Noni with a favorite liniment, and use as you would liniment.

- Try Noni-clay poultices. (See "Mixing Noni With Clay" on page 159.) Noni-clay can hasten recovery, draw out toxins and normalize cells. Try Noni-clay on swellings, sprains and internal injuries.

- Apply Noni fruit juice directly onto open wounds.

- Soak a cloth in Noni fruit juice and wrap the cloth around whatever part of the horse's leg requires treatment. For relatively large areas, or for a more economical treatment, use a mixture of equal parts Noni and water.

More about
Giving Noni to Horses:

If you consider that the average horse weighs about 1200 to 1500 pounds, almost ten times the weight of many adult people, you might think that horses would need about ten times the amount of Noni. But this is not so. In fact, horses seem to respond better to Noni than most people do. This may be because horses are naturally sensitive creatures, or because they do not harbor negative opinions or skepticism, which can inhibit a human's journey to greater health. In fact, too much Noni can make horses feel too good, which can make them difficult to manage.

SECTION 2

TOPICAL

APPLICATIONS

Topical applications of Noni fruit juice are surprisingly versatile. They are used not only for skin conditions, but also to help the body heal, repair and detoxify organs and other tissue in local areas. Noni can do this because of its unusual ability to reach through the skin to areas inside the body that need the Noni's healing compounds.

Applying Noni topically also draws to the treatment area the therapeutic effects of Noni taken orally. This gives you some control as to where you want Noni to work. For example, while your body may direct your oral doses of Noni to a condition it considers a priority, you may want to focus on another condition instead. So, you would apply topical applications to the area associated with that condition.

Because drinking Noni fruit juice enhances the effects of Topical Applications, it is always a good idea to combine the two.

141

Select a procedure for taking Noni orally from Section 1. Then choose the topical applications in Section 2 that are appropriate for your condition.

Topical Applications are also the answer when people are unable to drink Noni or when, as in the case of some children, they simply don't want to drink it.

This Section begins with a discussion of Noni Compresses and Poultices, Noni Poultice Paste, and Noni Clay. These Topical Applications have the most uses. The applications that follow are listed alphabetically.

37.

THE NONI COMPRESS

A Noni Compress is placed directly on the skin, to help conditions inside the body. It may be applied at room temperature or with an ice pack.

USE A NONI COMPRESS FOR:

- Athletic injuries.
- Carpal tunnel syndrome.
- Injuries and conditions of the bones and joints.
- Injuries and conditions that require cold therapeutic applications.

    (cont.)

- Painful areas.
- Sprains.
- Swelling and inflammation.
- To accelerate healing in areas where surgery has occurred.
- Tumors.
- Women's labia after child birth.

How to Make and
Apply a Noni Compress:

1. Select a compress pad large enough to cover the treatment area. Do not unfold gauze pads in order to cover a larger area. The pads will need to be several layers thick to hold enough Noni fruit juice. Use two pads side-by-side if necessary.

2. Pour a tablespoonful of Noni fruit juice into a bowl. A tablespoonful is sufficient for most 4" x 4" pads. This is a typical size for a Noni Compress. Refer to the information box on page 146, for amounts of Noni to use with various size pads.

3. Place the pad on the Noni fruit juice, and gently press down on the pad to help it soak up all the liquid. The side that has soaked up the liquid will have a layer of pulp on it.

4. When you remove the pad from the bowl, wipe up any pulp that remains in the bowl using the pulpy side of the pad.

5. Center the wet pad over the treatment area. The pulpy side should be touching the skin. The Compress will feel cold.

6. Cover the Compress with plastic wrap, and then with an old hand-towel. The plastic wrap and the towel will prevent your clothing from being stained by any Noni that may leak out. The plastic also keeps the compress moist. If it completely covers the compress pad, it can help keep the compress from dripping. If you prefer that the plastic wrap not touch your skin, simply fold the plastic so that it covers only the compress pad.

7. If you want to move around while wearing the Compress, secure the Compress to your body. Use whatever material works best for the area of the body that is wearing the Compress. For example, try using gauze bandage, first-aid tape, an ace bandage, a towel, or a bandanna. Be sure not to tie the Compress on too tightly.

MORE ABOUT
THE NONI COMPRESS:

Keep the Compress in place for a few hours, or overnight. Apply the Compress once or twice a day (or each night before bed), until the condition improves.

If a cold treatment is indicated, such as for sprains, wrap an ice pack in a thin towel and place it over the Compress.

If a skin rash or pimples erupt after using a Noni Compress, toxins are probably being released through the skin. Drink more purified water to help flush the toxins through the kidneys instead.

ABOUT COMPRESS PADS
(AND POULTICE PADS)

- Gauze pads and cheesecloth work well, but so do napkins and paper towels, which are more economical. Fold paper towels in half twice, so they are four layers thick.

- Rolled gauze can also be used. Unroll the gauze, then fold it three or four layers thick, to an appropriate size.

- To cover relatively large areas, use a facecloth.

- Use sterile gauze pads, preferably the non-stick variety, over open wounds.

Guidelines for How Much Liquid to Use With Various Sizes of Compress Pads and Poultice Pads

One 2" x 2" gauze pad	One-half tablespoonful
One 4" x 4" gauze pad	One tablespoonful
One paper towel folded in quarters	One tablespoonful
One paper napkin	One tablespoonful
Three paper napkins sandwiched together	One ounce
Three paper towels sandwiched together	One-and-a-half ounces
One face cloth	Three ounces

Note: These amount may vary depending on the thickness and absorbency of the material used.

38.

THE NONI
POULTICE

Noni Poultices are made with a mixture of Noni fruit juice and purified water that is also called a 1:1 Dilution.* The water provides a pathway for Noni's healing compounds to penetrate the body. Noni Poultices may be applied at room temperature or heated.

USE A NONI POULTICE FOR:

- Conditions that involve the internal organs.
- Conditions that require a heated application.
- Asthma, bronchitis, and other lung conditions.
- Diabetes (when placed over the pancreas).
  (cont.)

*Read More about how a 1:1 Dilution penetrates the body in my book, *Healing Secrets of Noni.*

- Endometriosis.
- Kidney and adrenal problems.
- Liver complaints.
- Mastitis.
- Menstrual cramps.
- Old injuries.
- Painful areas.
- Sluggish or malfunctioning organs.

How to Make and
Apply a Noni Poultice:

1. Select a poultice pad large enough to cover the treatment area. (If you are heating the Poultice using Method 1 on page 151, make the pad extra thick to help retain heat.)

2. Determine how much liquid you will need for the Poultice. The amount will depend on the size and thickness of the poultice pad you are using. See the information box on page 146 for ideas for how much liquid you may need for various size pads. Remember, half of this amount will be Noni, and half will be purified water.

3. Pour the amount of Noni fruit juice that you will need into a bowl. Measure an equal amount of purified water. Pour the water into the Noni fruit juice in a slow, steady, uninterrupted stream. Meanwhile, swirl the two liquids together, or stir them for several seconds.

4. Place the pad on the Noni fruit juice, and gently press down on the pad to help it soak up all the liquid.

5. When you remove the pad from the bowl, wipe up any pulp that remains in the bowl using the pulpy side of the pad.

6. Center the wet pad over the treatment area. The pulpy side should be touching the skin. (continued on page 150.)

How Noni Compresses and Poultices are Different

- Compresses are made of Noni fruit juice alone. Poultices contain equal parts of Noni and purified water.

- Compresses have a greater tendency to draw out toxins. Poultices have a greater tendency to move Noni's healing compounds more deeply into the body.

- Compresses are preferred for joint and bone conditions. Poultices are preferred for organ conditions.

- Compresses may be applied at room temperature or chilled with ice. Poultices may be applied at room temperature or heated.

- Compresses are preferred for smaller treatment areas. Poultices are more economical to apply to larger areas, because the volume of liquid used is partly water.

How Compresses and Poultices are Similar

- Both may be used for pain.

- Both may help accelerate healing, and improve flexibility and circulation in the treatment area.

- Both may soften the skin on which they are placed.

- Both may be placed over areas where the skin has been cut, scraped, or bruised, or that has a rash or other skin condition, but neither is meant specifically for skin conditions. For skin treatments, refer to the Topical Splash on page 235, or the Rash Plaster on page 221.

7. Cover the Poultice first with plastic wrap, then with an old hand-towel to protect your clothing from any Noni that may leak.

8. If you want to move around while wearing the Poultice, secure the Poultice to your body. Use whatever material works best for the area of the body that is wearing the Poultice. Try using a gauze bandage, first-aid tape, an ace bandage, a towel, or a bandanna. Be sure not to tie the Poultice on too tightly.

More about
Noni Poultices:

Keep the Poultice in place for several hours, or overnight.

Apply the Poultice once or twice a day (or each night before bed), until the condition improves.

Poultices can be applied hot. The heat may help Noni's healing compounds to be absorbed into the body. This chapter describes two methods for heating Noni Poultices.

Should I Use a Noni
Compress or Poultice?

If you are not sure which to use, ask yourself:

- Is the target area related to a bone, joint, or ligament? If so, use a Compress.

- Is the target area related to a muscle, soft tissue, or an internal organ? If so, use a Poultice.

- Would the target area benefit from a cold application? If so, use a Compress.

- Would the area feel better with heat? If so, use a Poultice.

- Is the ailment in the target area characterized by toxicity, swelling, or pus? If so, a Compress is preferred.

NONI POULTICE
HEATING METHOD 1

1. Prepare the Noni Poultice following Steps 1, 2, and 3 on page 148.

2. Pour the Noni-water mixture into a small glass or stainless steel pot. Put the pot on the stove over low heat.

3. Constantly stir the liquid, or swirl the pot to keep the liquid moving. Check its temperature often with your finger. Do not let the liquid simmer, boil, or become too hot to touch. If any portion of the juice is brought to too high a temperature, some of Noni's healing compounds will be destroyed.

4. When the Noni-water mixture is hot enough, remove the pot from the burner.

5. Lay the poultice pad on the liquid in the pot. Follow Steps 4 through 8 in the procedure for applying Noni Poultices. However, before you place the Poultice on your body, test its temperature to make sure it won't burn your skin.

6. Place a sheet of plastic wrap over the heated Poultice. Then cover it with a folded towel to help retain the heat.

Note:

- Do not use an aluminum pot.

- Do not use a microwave oven.

- Do not heat undiluted Noni fruit juice. If Noni is mixed with water and then heated, its healing compounds are less likely to be destroyed.

Heating Method 2

Use this heating method when you want the heat to last as long as possible.

1. Apply the Poultice to the body following Steps 1 through 7 on pages 148-150. The Poultice will feel cold on contact, but it will heat up immediately once a hot towel is applied, as follows.

2. Immerse a towel in a pot of heated water.

3. Wearing rubber gloves for protection, wring out the hot water. Fold the towel so that it will cover the Poultice.

4. Test the towel's temperature to make sure that it won't be too hot for the person receiving it. If it is, let it cool for a few minutes before applying, or put a dry towel between the Poultice and the heated towel.

5. Place the hot towel over the Poultice.

Note: The towel can be reheated and reapplied without removing the Poultice.

39.

NONI
POULTICE PASTE

This is a form of concentrated Noni that includes the Noni pulp, and that is excellent for topical applications.

TRY NONI POULTICE PASTE FOR:

- Athletic injuries.
- Blisters.
- Bruises.
- Burns.
- Canker sores.
- Cuts and wounds.
- Herpes.
  (cont.)

153

- Joint pain in relatively small areas.
- Mosquito bites
- Sore Nail cuticles.
- Sore throat.
- Sunburn
- Wrist pain, Carpal Tunnel Syndrome.

Also,

- For the Noni Hand Treatment 2 (page 205).
- For conditions that can be aided by topical ointments.
- And as a poultice to soothe ailing organs.

The above list comprises but a few of the many applications of Noni Paste. Hopefully they will inspire your imagination to try the Paste on other conditions as they arise.

How to Make
Noni Poultice Paste:

Before you begin, turn the bottle of Noni fruit juice upside-down then right-side up a few times. This will mix the pulp, which tends to settle to the bottom of the bottle, with the more watery portion of the juice.

1. Pour one ounce of Noni fruit juice into a bowl.

2. Let the bowl sit uncovered and outside the refrigerator for several hours or longer.

3. Allow enough water to evaporate until the Noni has become a thick paste. It should have the consistency of apple butter. You will know when enough water has evaporated when you tip the bowl and the Noni stays in place.

This recipe makes about one-and-a-half teaspoonfuls of Noni Paste. Double or triple the recipe as needed.

MORE ABOUT
MAKING NONI POULTICE PASTE:

Cover any unused Poultice Paste with plastic wrap and store it in the refrigerator.

It is important to monitor the Noni fruit juice while it is becoming Noni Paste. If you let too much water evaporate from the Noni, it will dry out. When this happens, Noni's therapeutic value is lost. Dried Noni does not reconstitute when you add water. You will have to start over again with fresh Noni fruit juice.

How fast Noni fruit juice will become Noni Poultice Paste depends on the humidity in the air. In dry climates, it may take only a few hours. In normal humidity it may take overnight or longer. If you live in a very humid climate, you may be unable to make Noni Paste indoors. An alternative is to place the Noni fruit juice in sunlight. Doing so can vitalize the Noni Paste with the sun's energy. However, in sunlight, evaporation can happen very quickly, so be sure to keep a close eye on it. It would also be wise to cover the bowl of Noni with a wire screen, or something similar that would keep out insects but still allow evaporation to occur.

Besides humidity, room temperature also plays a role in making Noni Paste. Noni can be left out for two days if the room temperature is below seventy degrees Fahrenheit. If the Noni rests for too long in a room much warmer than this, it can ferment and lose its therapeutic value. However, since you will not be ingesting Noni Paste, you can leave it out longer than you might if you were eventually going to drink it.

Do not try to evaporate the water from Noni using the stove. The temperature at which the water in the Noni fruit juice would steam away is high enough to destroy its healing compounds.

How to Use
Noni Poultice Paste:

For conditions on the skin:

1. Apply enough paste to cover the affected area.

2. Allow the Paste to air-dry or cover it. If the area is relatively large, you could cover it with plastic wrap. If it is relatively small, use an adhesive bandage.

For conditions inside the body:
Noni Poultice Paste can also be used topically to treat conditions inside the body (such as ailing joints and organs).

1. Locate the area on your body closest to the organ you wish to treat.

2. Make enough Poultice Paste to cover the chosen area with Paste at least one-eighth of an inch thick.

3. Spread the Paste over the chosen area. Cover the area with plastic wrap to prevent the Noni from staining your clothes, linens, or furniture.

4. Keep the Paste in place for at least an hour. Unless your condition would be aggravated by heat, feel free to increase the penetration of Noni's healing compounds into the body by placing a heating pad over the plastic-covered Paste.

More about
Using Noni Poultice Paste:

Noni Poultice Paste has advantages over Noni Compresses (page 143) and Poultices (page 147). The Paste is easier to apply and much less messy because it won't drip like the juice will. You can apply a thick coat of Noni Paste over an area, thus giving that area more Noni healing compounds per square inch than is possible with Noni compresses. This makes Noni Paste especially helpful for small areas.

On the other hand, the advantages of Noni Compresses or Poultices include: they can be applied immediately—you don't have to wait a day to make Noni Paste, and they distribute Noni's healing compounds more evenly over a larger area. In addition, it is better to apply Noni Compresses or Poultices over skin that is wounded or that has a rash. The concentrated Noni pulp may irritate the skin in these cases. And because the pulp would adhere to the broken skin, it would be more difficult to wash off. It would also be more likely to stain the skin purple.

If your condition is associated with high toxicity, as in some tumors, you may prefer to keep the Poultice Paste uncovered. As the Paste dries out, it emphasizes the Noni's ability to draw toxins from the body. However, if your intention is specifically to draw out toxins, try Noni-clay (page 159) instead.

A Word on
Natural Healing Methods:

This chapter seems like a good place to point out how natural healing methods, such as Noni, do not work like drugs. This is important to understand so that your expectations of Noni are reasonable, and that you can better identify and appreciate the effects that Noni does have.

Sometimes, topical applications of Noni can indeed ease pain as if you had taken a pain-killer. But this doesn't always occur, in which case the benefits of Noni may be less apparent or take longer to notice. This is because the condition is being healed from within. For example, after two days of a severe sore throat, I decided to cover my neck with Noni Paste overnight. In the morning, I noticed my throat was still sore but in the next few hours I began coughing up dark, thick phlegm. The more I coughed up, the less painful my throat was. The Noni did not remove my symptoms immediately, but helped my body address a truer cause of the sore throat.

40.

NONI-CLAY

This is like a biological sponge for pain, toxins, and malaise.

TRY MIXING NONI WITH CLAY FOR:

Conditions whose congestion or toxic overload is apparent, such as:

- Abscesses.
- Swelling.
- Tumors.

Conditions whose toxic or excess-energy overload may not be as apparent, such as:

- Arthritis.
- Fever.
- Headaches.
- Heavy metal poisoning.
  (cont.)

- Injuries.
- Lung conditions.
- Rheumatism.
- Sinusitis.

And, when you want to access and release the emotional energy attached to local conditions.

HOW TO
MIX NONI WITH CLAY:

1. Measure one part of powdered clay and put it into a bowl.
2. Add one part purified water.
3. Add one part Noni fruit juice.
4. Mix the ingredients together into a paste using a non-metal spoon.

MORE ABOUT
MIXING NONI WITH CLAY:

How much is "one part" of each of the above ingredients can vary from one tablespoonful to several ounces. It depends on the size of the area you wish to treat. Noni-clay mixtures should be applied directly onto the chosen area.

Areas that are relatively small (such as fingers, small bruises, wrists), should be covered with a layer of Noni-clay one-eighth inch thick. Areas that take up about a few square inches (knees, ankles, neck), should have a layer one-quarter inch thick. Relatively large areas (liver, lungs, lower abdomen), should be covered with Noni-clay one-half inch thick. In each case, the Noni-clay application should be wide enough to cover the affected area. Also, the deeper inside the body the condition lies, and the more serious the condition, the thicker the Noni-clay application should be.

Several kinds of dried clay are available in health food stores. Choose the least expensive for the topical applications described in this chapter. Dried clay can also be bought from ceramics supplies stores. Ask for "virgin" clay—clay that has not undergone any treatment since it was extracted from the quarry.

Use a plastic or wooden spoon to mix the Noni and clay. Metal can interfere with the charged particles in the clay, thus making the treatment less effective.[19]

HOW TO USE
NONI-CLAY MIXTURES:

METHOD 1

1. Identify the area you want to treat.

2. Using a wooden spoon, apply enough Noni-clay mixture to cover the chosen area to the suggested thickness. Use the back of the spoon to smooth the Noni-clay to a relatively even thickness.

3. When you are finished, remove the Noni clay with a spoon and throw it away. (For removing Noni-clay, you can use a metal spoon.) Wipe the area with a damp cloth, or wash off the remaining Noni-clay in the shower.

METHOD 2

1. Identify the area you want to treat.

2. Cut a single layer of cheesecloth large enough to cover the chosen area, plus about four inches. Center it on the area to be treated.

3. Using a wooden spoon, spread enough Noni-clay mixture over the cheesecloth to cover the chosen area to the thickness suggested above. There should be about two inches of cheesecloth leftover around all the edges. Use the back of the spoon to smooth the Noni-clay to a relatively even thickness.

4. Cover the Noni-clay with another layer or two of cheesecloth.

5. When you are finished, remove the poultice by lifting the cheesecloth. Throw it in the trash. Wipe up the Noni-clay that remains in the area with a damp cloth.

Method 1 is probably more effective because the Noni-clay lies directly on the skin. It is the method of choice if you have less than an hour to keep the Noni-clay in place. On the downside, it is harder to remove the Noni-clay, and you may need to take a shower to remove it completely.

Method 2 is preferred when you want to remove the Noni-clay quickly and with a minimum of clean-up. This may be especially helpful when treating children and when you need to alternate Noni-clay placement locations. However, the layer of cheesecloth puts a barrier between the Noni-clay and the body, which may reduce the treatment's beneficial effects.

Here are some suggestions for specific Noni-clay applications:

- For headaches, apply Noni-clay alternately to the nape of the neck and then the forehead for about one hour each. Continue to alternate these applications until the pain is gone.[20]

- For fevers, apply Noni-clay to the lower abdomen. Remove the clay when it becomes warm.[21]

- For arthritis, apply Noni-clay to the afflicted area to draw out the toxins and metabolic wastes that have pooled around the joints causing inflammation and pain.

- To help rid the mouth of mercury and other heavy metals, spread Noni-clay on the cheeks. This will also serve as a Noni facial, and do wonders for your skin. Follow with a favorite moisturizer.

- For sinusitis, try Noni-clay on the forehead and upper cheeks. Also apply Noni-clay over the liver.

MORE ABOUT
USING NONI-CLAY MIXTURES:

If rashes, eruptions, or itching occurs during a Noni-clay application, remove the Noni-clay. These effects are likely the result of toxins being pulled from inside the body, which are attracted by the clay. However, these effects are less likely to occur when Noni is used in combination with the clay.

Noni-clay applications should be left in place for two to four hours; however, they can also be applied before bed and removed in the morning. Daily applications should be sufficient. But if the Noni-clay applications are easing pain, they can be applied more frequently.

If you wish to keep the Noni-clay in place overnight, you will need to cover it with plastic wrap to protect your linens. However, if you are applying the Noni-clay in order to draw toxins from the body, it is better to keep the Noni-clay uncovered. The process of drawing out toxins and excesses from the body seems to correlate with the clay drying out. For pain and injuries, I have found the clay works just as well covered or uncovered.

Clay poultices are known for their ability to draw toxins from the body. Adding Noni to the clay lends an "intelligence" to this process that regulates it and makes the release more harmonious and soothing. Adding Noni also allows the emotional energy associated with the condition to be released. This doesn't usually happen when using clay alone. With Noni, cycles of toxin release and emotion release may alternate.

It is also effective to apply Noni-clay to areas that are slow to heal. Sometimes the delay is due to unresolved emotions associated with the disease or the original trauma. Noni-clay can help release these old, pent-up emotions. Don't be surprised if you start to feel some of these emotions, no matter where on the body the Noni-clay may be placed. Emotions are usually connected in some way to all our pains and illnesses. If the emotions are not released as the condition heals, then recovery can be inhibited.

During the emotional-release cycle, try to remember that these are old emotions coming forward. They are trying to find release. Although these emotions may feel very "real," they are not necessarily real in present time. So try to be as objective about them as possible. Cry your heart out if you need to, but cry only for as long as you have to. Take the first window given to stop.

Crying likes to perpetuate itself. During the process of crying, a moment comes when we have finished crying about a particular thing. Then we have a choice to stop crying. But the heart likes to take advantage of the release, and usually finds something else to cry about, and so we start to cry for a different reason. If you think that the Noni-clay has stimulated a release of an old emotion, keep the crying focused on that one emotion. Give yourself permission to stop crying as soon as you no longer feel that one emotion. If several old emotions surface, be careful to let each one go as soon as the release finally occurs and the crying cycle stops. You will know when this occurs because your energy will feel a sense of relief, you will feel emotionally spent, you will regain a sense of inner peace, or your entire outlook on life will improve.

It is also possible to release emotions without having to process them through crying. If you would like to try this, here is a technique that might help: When you feel an emotion swell up inside, imagine it is contained inside soap bubbles. As the bubbles rise up, they pass out of your body. Imagine them floating upwards into the sky. Because the bubbles encase the emotion, you are protected from having to feel the full force of that emotion.

If you try this technique, it helps to keep a notepad with you. As emotions arise, write down each one as you sense it bubbling up. See how long a list you can make. You may notice several flavors of a particular emotion, so use adjectives freely when you make your list. For example, you might write: "deep sadness, gut-wrenching sadness, bittersweet sadness, mild sadness," etc. Watch how emotions may alternate or repeat themselves. Each time a certain one comes up you may be releasing it at a deeper level. Writing down these emotions also allows you to identify them, to forgive the circumstances and people involved, and then to move on. When each emotion-bubble passes out of your body, cross it off your list. Doing so symbolizes its release.

41.

Noni After-Shave

A soothing solution.

Use Noni After-Shave:

- As you would regular after-shave: on the face, legs, or under-arms.
- For skin that gets irritated or dry from shaving.

How to Make and
Apply Noni After-Shave:

1. Pour one ounce of Noni fruit juice into a small container with a lid.

2. Measure three tablespoonfuls (one-and-a-half ounces) of purified water. Add this entire amount of water to the Noni

167

in a slow, steady, uninterrupted stream. Meanwhile, swirl the liquids together for several seconds. This amount of After-shave should be enough for several shaves.

3. After shaving, apply the Noni-water mixture to the skin with a cotton ball or with your hands.

4. Allow the liquid to air dry on your skin. Reapply if your skin is particularly irritated.

MORE ABOUT THE
NONI AFTER-SHAVE:

Don't shake the Noni fruit juice bottle before pouring Noni for After-shave. The more watery part of the juice, found at the top of a new bottle of Noni (which has been left undisturbed), is better for After-shave because it is less pulpy.

Except in hot climates, the Noni After-shave may be left at room temperature for a couple of days. Otherwise, store the Noni After-shave in the refrigerator for your next use.

Noni fruit juice can be sticky if applied directly to the skin. This is why it is suggested to mix it with water. One-and-a-half parts of water to one part of Noni fruit juice is strong enough to be effective, without being sticky. This mixture of Noni and water is also called a 2:3 Dilution.

If you have been nicked by the razor blade and are bleeding, apply extra Noni After-shave to the cut with a tissue or cotton ball and apply pressure. The bleeding should stop faster with Noni.

Noni After-shave also helps to soften and smooth the skin.

42.

THE NONI
BACK COMPRESS

The Noni Back Compress may consist of one compress pad or two separate ones, depending on the application area.

A NONI BACK COMPRESS
MAY BE HELPFUL FOR:

- Broken ribs.
- Low back pain.
- Muscle spasms.
- Pinched nerves.
- Sore hips.
- Sore shoulders.
- Spinal subluxations.

How to Make and Apply
A Noni Back Compress:

1. Have the person who is to receive the Noni Back Compress lie on his or her stomach.

2. If massage does not cause additional discomfort, massage the painful area for a few minutes to increase circulation.

3. Decide if you will need one or two compress pads and what size they should be:

   • If the pain is over the spine, you will need one compress pad to cover the painful area.

   • If the pain is elsewhere, say, on the hip, ribs, or shoulder, then you will need two separate compress pads.

      • One will cover the painful area.

      • The other will cover the portion of the spine that is closest to the painful area. Back pain is closely related to the spine. Spinal subluxations may be contributing to the pain, and the pain may be contributing to spinal subluxations. The second compress pad, placed over the spine, addresses any connection that the painful area may have with the spine.

4. Make the compress pads. Each will consist of three paper napkins sandwiched together. (You could use another material, but I prefer napkins because they are the perfect size for this purpose.)

5. Pour an ounce of Noni fruit juice into a bowl.

6. Place a compress pad on the Noni fruit juice, and gently press down on the pad to help it soak up the liquid. When you remove the pad from the bowl, wipe up any Noni pulp that remains in the bowl using the pulpy side of the pad.

7. Center the Back Compress over the painful area, with the pulpy side touching the skin.

8. If the Back Compress starts to drip, place a fourth napkin over it to soak up the excess juice. If you need a second

compress pad, add another ounce of Noni to the bowl. Soak another sandwich of three paper napkins in the Noni and center this compress pad over the portion of the spine closest to the painful area.

MORE ABOUT THE NONI BACK COMPRESS:

If the individual needs to move around, you will have to secure the Back Compress to the torso. Here is one way to do that. Cover the compress with plastic wrap, and then with an old towel. Wrap an ace bandage or gauze bandage around the torso about three times, covering as much of the compress as possible. The bandage should be just tight enough to hold everything in place. In case the compress leaks, the individual should wear old clothing because Noni will stain.

If the individual to receive the Back Compress is sensitive to plastic, use old towels instead.

Apply the Noni Back Compress at least once a day. Even after the pain goes away, continue daily treatments for a few days, to help avoid relapse. The Back Compress may be worn for several hours or overnight.

Paper napkins are the perfect size compress pads for Noni Back Compresses. Use sterile gauze pads if the skin to be covered is broken or has a rash.

The naturally cold temperature of Noni Compresses made with refrigerated Noni fruit juice provides an analgesic effect, in addition to the analgesic effect of the Noni itself.

For sudden and painful back conditions, take a Trauma Dose (page 85) in addition to the Noni Back Compress.

43.

Noni to Enhance Sleep and Dreams

I dream of Noni.

Try this Technique to:

- Enhance dream recall.
- Help you fall asleep at bedtime.

How to Use Noni
To Enhance Sleep and Dreams:

1. Before you go to bed at night, prepare the following mixture of Noni and water, which is also called a 1:4 Dilution:

   a. Measure one ounce of Noni fruit juice and pour it into a drinking glass.

   b. Use a one-cup measuring cup to measure four ounces of purified water.

   c. Swirl the Noni by moving the glass in a circular motion. Keep swirling, and add the water in a slow, steady, uninterrupted stream. Continue to swirl the mixture for a few more seconds.

2. Pour about one teaspoonful of the Noni-water mixture into a small bowl. Press a cotton ball into the Noni. Put the bowl and the glass of remaining Noni-water mixture beside your bed.

3. Spread an old towel over your pillow, to protect your pillowcase from getting stained if the cotton ball falls on it.

4. When you are ready for bed, drink some (or all if you like) of the Noni-water mixture in the glass.

5. Lift the cotton ball out of the Noni and squeeze out any excess liquid. The cotton ball should be wet but not dripping wet.

6. Place the cotton ball in the center of your forehead, just above the bony ridge of your eyebrows. The pulpy side of the cotton should be touching your skin. Gently press the cotton ball against your forehead to help it adhere to your skin.

7. Lay down on your back, close your eyes, and focus on the relatively cool temperature of the Noni on your forehead. Pay attention to how the Noni warms with your body-heat over time. This in itself can be very relaxing. Allow yourself to drift off to sleep.

More about Using Noni
To Enhance Sleep and Dreams:

A cotton ball made of pure cotton is preferable to "cosmetic puffs," which look like cotton balls but are made of synthetic fiber. Cotton holds more Noni than synthetic fiber does, and is less likely to drip. It also tends to adhere to the skin better.

If you tend to toss and turn when you sleep, or if you prefer to sleep on your side or stomach, you will need to secure the cotton ball to your forehead. Try various ways, such as a bandanna, first-aid tape, a headband, or even a nightcap, to find out which works best for you. However, you don't have to keep the cotton ball in place all night long. After it helps you fall asleep, it doesn't matter if the cotton ball remains on your forehead or not. You could also try keeping the cotton ball on your forehead only for as long as you can lie comfortably on your back. When you need to change positions, return the cotton ball to the bowl. The relatively short amount of time the Noni stays in place may be just enough to help you sleep.

Please follow very carefully the recipe for making the Noni-water mixture, as described in Step 1. Doing so will release certain energetic properties of Noni* that bring harmony and balance to the nervous system. When a cotton ball soaked with this mixture is placed in the center of the forehead, balance and harmony is brought to the brain, and in particular, to the pineal gland. This can help you relax—hopefully enough to fall asleep.

If drinking Noni tends to keep you awake at night, you may prefer to omit Step 4. However, the effects of this mixture of Noni and water are different than those of undiluted Noni. Drinking at least a few sips of this mixture before bed may promote sleep as it helps calm down an over-stressed nervous system.

---

*You can read more about the energetic effects of Noni in, *Healing Secrets of Noni.*

The area in the center of the forehead on which the Noni-soaked cotton ball is placed, is also called a "chakra." Chakras are centers of energy in the body. The forehead chakra is associated with the mind's eye, and is sometimes referred to as the "window" to one's inner worlds or dream worlds. When a 1:4 Dilution is placed on a chakra center, it promotes balance and harmony in that chakra. This allows the chakra to gently open if it has been closed, or to open wider with greater strength and confidence if it has been only somewhat open. Since clear dream recall is often associated with an open forehead chakra, performing this technique can help you remember your dreams.

Many people like to remember their dreams because they have found that dreams are a source of truth. Through dreams they can find answers, insights, and guidance. If you would like to try getting an answer from your dreams, try this simple technique:

1. Before bed, write down a question that you would like to receive insight about from your dreams. Copy the same question a few more times, so it is written down at least three times. This will imprint the question in your consciousness.

2. Perform the Noni Technique to Enhance Sleep and Dreams.

3. As you drift off to sleep, expect to have a dream that will address the question that you wrote down.

4. When you wake up, whether in the morning or in the middle of the night, write down whatever dream you remember. At this point, do not try to edit your writing or figure out your dream—just write it down. If you don't remember any dreams, write down how you feel. If you don't sense any particular emotions, ask yourself what you KNOW about the answer to your question. Write this down.

5. Sometime later that day or that night, read what you wrote down. Look for a connection between the question you asked and the dream that you received.

THE NONI
EYE POULTICE

A Noni Eye Poultice can be helpful for a variety of eye conditions as well as vision problems, for it raises the overall health of the eyes.

USE A NONI EYE POULTICE FOR:

- Eyestrain.
- Glaucoma.
- Headaches behind the eyes.
- Macular degeneration.

    (cont.)

- Pain in the eyes.
- Pink eye and other eye and eyelid infections.
- Sties.
- Vision problems.
- Injuries, after first aid has been applied.
- Also, after eye surgery to promote recovery.

How to Make and
Apply a Noni Eye Poultice:

1. Make an Eye Poultice pad using sterile gauze. It should be two inches wide and about six inches long. It should also be four layers thick. You could unroll twenty-four inches of two-inch wide gauze bandage and fold it to fit these measurements. Or you could use a 4" x 4" sterile gauze pad: Unfold the pad once, refold it lengthwise, then cut two inches off one end.

2. Pour one tablespoonful of Noni fruit juice into a bowl. Measure a tablespoonful of purified water, and add this to the Noni. Stir the liquids together.

3. Press the poultice pad into the Noni-water mixture until it becomes wet. Then lift the pad up. Hold the pad over the bowl, and gently squeeze out the excess liquid. The pad should be wet, but not soaking wet. We don't want the Noni to drip down your face when the Eye Poultice is applied.

4. Lie down, holding the Eye Poultice. Place the center of the pad over the bridge of your nose. The pulpy side of the pad should be next to your skin.

5. Close your eyes. Cover your eyes with the rest of the pad. Gently press the pad over your eyeballs and into the corners of your eyes, to conform the pad to the contours of your face.

6. Rest with the Eye Poultice in place for twenty to thirty minutes, or until the pad dries out. You could also apply the Eye Poultice just before going to sleep at night. If necessary, use a bandanna to hold the pad in place.

More about the
Noni Eye Poultice:

Some of the Noni-water mixture may seep into your eyes. This can enhance the therapeutic effect of the Noni Eye Poultice. To allow more liquid under your eyelids, gently press the Poultice into the inside corners of your eyes while you roll your eyes in circles.

If some of the Noni-water mixture gets into your eyes it may sting, but it may not. Interestingly, you may feel the sting at some times and not others. Whether Noni will sting or not depends on the person, the type of eye condition, and how the eyes may be feeling on that particular day.

For infections and serious conditions on the lid or the skin near the eye, you can use a Noni Compress (page 143) on the eye. Follow the directions for making a Noni Eye Poultice, but instead use undiluted Noni fruit juice (as you would when making Noni Compresses.) Water is added to a Noni Eye Poultice when you wish to treat a condition of the eye or inside the eye itself. The extra moisture that the water provides allows you to press the poultice pad against the eyes, thus releasing the Noni-water mixture into the eyes. This should not be done with undiluted Noni because any pulpy material that gets in the eye can cause further irritation. There is enough water in a Noni Eye Poultice that the pulp tends to stay trapped in the poultice pad, and only the Noni-water is released.

Expect some Noni pulp to remain on your face when you remove the Eye Poultice. This wipes off easily with a wet facecloth.

The Noni Eye Poultice may help to relieve pain. If you are using it for this purpose, wring out the poultice pad when it gets warm from your body heat. Re-soak the pad in more Noni-water solution, and reapply. The cool temperature of the Noni can enhance the Noni's own analgesic effect.

The Noni Eye Poultice can be very soothing and relaxing. If used regularly, the Eye Poultice may prevent headaches due to eyestrain.

179

A 2" x 6" poultice pad will fit most adults. Children will need a smaller size. If you are treating only one eye, use a poultice pad that is about 2" x 3" in size.

To enhance the benefit of the Noni Eye Poultice, drink a dose of Noni fruit juice just before the Eye Poultice is applied. Drinking Noni will enhance the beneficial effects of Noni applied topically.

THE NONI FACIAL

Add the Noni Facial to your daily routine to help keep your skin feeling youthful and glowing.

THE NONI FACIAL
CAN BE HELPFUL FOR:

- Acne and Pimples.
- Aging skin.
- Blotchy skin.
- Dry skin.
- Helping the skin stay youthful.
- Rashes on the face.
- Reducing stress.
- Relaxing the facial muscles.
- Wrinkled skin.

How to Make and
Apply a Noni Facial:

1. Wash your face using your usual cleansing program.

2. Pour about one tablespoonful of Noni fruit juice in a bowl.

3. Cut up three strips of gauze bandage or cheesecloth. Two should be large enough to cover each side of your face and one should cover your neck. Or you could use several smaller pieces.

4. Gently press one strip of gauze into the Noni fruit juice until it is wet. Lift the wet gauze and hold it over the bowl. Squeeze it gently to remove excess juice.

5. Place the wet gauze on one side of your face, with the pulpy side next to your skin. Repeat with the other pieces of gauze until your entire face is covered. Include your forehead, cheeks, nose, and chin. You can also treat your neck if you wish. The surface tension of the wet gauze will keep the gauze sticking to your face and neck.

6. Fold a facecloth in half, and soak it in hot tap water.

7. Wring out the excess water from the facecloth. Lay the folded facecloth over the left or right side of your face. Hold it there for a few minutes until the facecloth cools. (This feels absolutely wonderful!)

8. Wring out the facecloth and soak it again in the hot water. Wring out the excess water and lay the folded facecloth over the other side of your face. Repeat this process for your neck. You may apply the heated facecloth to your neck and to each side of your face a second time.

9. Remove the gauze and rinse your face and neck with cold water. Wipe off any Noni pulp that remains on your skin.

10. Apply an astringent to close the pores. Or, apply cold Noni After-shave (page 167) using a cotton ball. Then apply a favorite moisturizing cream.

MORE ABOUT
THE NONI FACIAL:

If someone else is applying the Noni Facial on you, they may use three heated facecloths to cover your entire face and neck at once.

Use facecloths that you don't mind staining with Noni fruit juice.

If your tap water is heavily chlorinated, you may prefer to use heated purified water.

It is okay to cover the eyes with the gauze. (But you probably won't be able to do this if you are giving the Noni Facial to yourself.)

The heat may make your face red and possibly blotchy. This is temporary. If your normal skin color doesn't return as soon as you'd like, do the Noni Facial before bed. Or, try using water that is not as hot.

The gauze strips can be washed and reused for future Noni Facials.

Try the Noni Facial with only one side of your face to discover for yourself the difference just one treatment can make!

THE NONI
FINGER SOAK

This procedure may be used for one or more fingers.

USE THE NONI
FINGER SOAK FOR:

- Arthritis.
- Fungus.
- Infections.
- Injuries.
- Insect stings.
- Joint pain.
- Nail and cuticle conditions.

- Neuralgia.
- Stiffness.

How to Make and
Apply the Noni Finger Soak:

1. Find a bowl that is large enough to fit all your fingers. (If you bend your hand slightly at the knuckles, and place your hand in the bowl knuckles first, then the tops of your fingers should rest comfortably on the bottom of the bowl.)

2. Measure a tablespoonful of Noni fruit juice. Hold the finger to be treated over the bowl. Pour the Noni fruit juice over your finger to coat it completely. Treat the entire finger, even if you have pain in only one part of it.

3. Massage the juice into the skin. (If your finger has been injured or if massage is painful, omit this step.)

    With the thumb and forefinger of the other hand, squeeze up and down the affected finger, along its top and bottom, then right and left sides.

    Periodically, run the finger across the bottom of the bowl in order to pick up some of the Noni pulp that has fallen into the bowl. This will re-coat the affected finger.

    Spend a few minutes massaging each finger that you want to treat. (This treatment may feel so soothing, that you will want to massage all your fingers.)

4. Remove your hand from the bowl and fill the bowl with hot purified water. The exact amount is not important. The water will naturally mix with the Noni that is already in the bowl. Test the temperature, then replace your fingers in the Noni-water liquid. Continue to massage your fingers, or let them rest in the bowl.

5. After a few minutes, the Noni-water liquid in the bowl will cool off. You may reheat it on the stove for a second Finger Soak. Heat it gently; don't let the Noni-water liquid simmer or boil.

MORE ABOUT
THE NONI FINGER SOAK:

Do not heat the water in a microwave.

Test the hot water before putting a child's fingers into it.

Like other Noni applications, the Finger Soak can help reduce pain, promote healing, and increase flexibility.

The skin on your fingers may become temporarily wrinkled from being in the water. Your skin may also feel dry afterwards. If it does, apply a favorite moisturizer.

46.

Noni
First Aid for
Minor Wounds

The information in this chapter is meant to supplement—not re-place—the procedures you might read in a First Aid handbook.

> When treating emergency situations—even minor ones—it is essential to use common sense and call upon the help of an Emergency Medical Team if necessary.

Noni can be Helpful for:

- Abrasions and scrapes.
- Bee stings and insect bites.
- Bleeding.
- Blows and bruises.
- Burns.
- Cuts.

How to use Noni
For bleeding wounds:

1. If there is no foreign object in the wound, cover the wound with a clean, absorbent material, and apply pressure.[22]

2. If no bones have been broken in the wounded area, raise the wound above the level of the heart to slow the blood flow.[23]

3. Try to calm the one who has been hurt. Assess how serious the wound is, what other injuries may be present, and if you need to call for help.[24]

4. As soon as possible pour Noni fruit juice over the wound, then continue to apply pressure. Make an impromptu Noni Compress (page 143) by quickly pouring some Noni onto the cloth you are using to apply pressure over the wound. Continue to apply pressure until the bleeding stops.

5. Give a Trauma Dose (page 85) to the injured person as soon as possible. Give Noni orally ONLY if the individual is awake, able to drink, and not in shock.[25]

6. Soak a non-stick gauze pad in Noni fruit juice. Apply the pulpy side of the pad on the wound. Adhere the pad to the body with first aid tape. Replace the gauze pad as soon as it dries.

   When you remove the pad, you may find that the Noni pulp has caked onto the wound. It will wash off naturally in the shower, or when the wound has healed enough. Don't pick off the Noni pulp because it is helping the body to form a scab.

Use non-stick gauze pads, because they won't interfere with the scab. A regular gauze pad, when removed, can pull the scab off.

Note: Every time I have used Noni for bleeding wounds, I have been surprised by how quickly Noni has helped stop the bleeding. I have also found that the sooner Noni is applied to a wound, the faster the wound seems to heal, and the sooner pain is alleviated.

How to use Noni for
Wounds that have Stopped Bleeding:

Noni fruit juice can stain wounded flesh a purplish color. The discoloration can remain for a while even after the wound has closed. To avoid this, the following procedure is suggested.

1. Clean the wound with an antiseptic other than Noni and cover it with an adhesive bandage to protect it.

2. Apply a Noni Compress over healthy skin adjacent to the wound. The Compress should be at least one inch wide and at least the same length as the wound. The body will transport Noni's healing compounds across body tissue to the wounded area where they are needed.

How to use Noni
For Blows and Bruises

1. Cut a piece of gauze large enough to cover the wound.

2. Soak the gauze in Noni. Then place it over the wound with the pulpy side of the gauze next to the skin.

3. Secure the gauze with an adhesive bandage or other material.

4. Apply an ice pack over the wound to help with the pain. Give a Trauma Dose (page 85), if the individual is awake and not in shock.[26]

How to use Noni
For Bee Stings and Insect Bites:

1. Soak a cotton ball in Noni and place it on the sting. If the sting is very painful, give the individual a Trauma Dose (page 85).

2. When the cotton ball gets warm from body heat, and if the sting is still painful, squeeze out the Noni. Soak the cotton in more Noni fruit juice and reapply. Do this as often as you need to for pain.

3. Replace the cotton with a fresh piece soaked in Noni. Place it over the sting. Place a small gauze pad or piece of paper towel over the cotton to soak up any excess liquid. Secure the cotton ball in place with first aid tape.

How to use Noni
For Minor Burns:

1. Immediately put the burned area under slow-running cold tap water.[27]

2. Pour refrigerated Noni fruit juice on the burn as soon as possible. (Refrigerated Noni is preferable because it is cold. But Noni at room temperature is better than none at all.)

3. If possible, submerge the burned area in Noni fruit juice. Otherwise, soak a non-fluffy material such as a non-stick gauze pad or handkerchief in Noni and place it over the burn.

   When the material gets warm from body heat, squeeze out and discard the Noni. Soak the material in more Noni and reapply.

4. Soak the material in Noni once more and place it over the burn. Place another gauze pad or piece of a paper towel over the compress to soak up any excess liquid. To secure the compress and the extra gauze pad in place, use first aid tape if the burn is small and you can adhere the tape to healthy skin. Otherwise use another cloth or gauze bandage.

5. Give the individual a Trauma Dose (page 85). Give Noni orally ONLY if the individual is awake, able to drink, and not in shock.[28]

• If you need to transport a burn victim to the emergency room, keep the burn covered with a cloth soaked in Noni.

• Some of the healing compounds in Noni fruit juice have proved to be very effective for helping the body heal quickly from burns, according to Dr. Ralph Heinicke, who has studied these compounds since the early 1970s.[29]

In the case of burns, be generous with the amount of Noni fruit juice that you apply. Have extra paper towels handy to soak up any excess juice that drips off the body.

THE NONI
FOOT BATH 1

If you cannot reach your feet, you will need someone to help you perform this procedure.

USE THE NONI FOOT BATH FOR
A VARIETY OF FOOT CONDITIONS INCLUDING:

- Arthritis.
- Athlete's foot.
- Blisters.
- Bone spurs.
- Bunions.
- Calluses.

- Cold feet.
- Dry skin.
- Gout.
- Poor circulation.
- Sore feet.

How to Apply a
Noni Foot Bath:

First, an overview of this procedure: You will be placing your foot in a plastic bag that contains Noni fruit juice. Then you will be inserting your foot, with the bag around it, in a tub of hot water.

1. Find a plastic bag suitable for this procedure. A one-gallon plastic recloseable bag will fit most feet. Recloseable bags are preferable to regular plastic bags, because they tend to be stronger. If your feet are too large to fit in a one-gallon bag, you can use a small plastic garbage bag.

   You will need two bags if you are treating both feet.

2. Pour some Noni fruit juice in the plastic bag.

   Here are some guidelines about how much juice you should use in each bag:

   • If you are treating your toes, or the sole of your foot, use one tablespoonful per bag.

   • If you are treating the entire foot, use one ounce per bag.

   • If you are treating your ankles, use two ounces of Noni. (Or, instead of using two ounces of Noni, you could put one ounce of Noni and one ounce of purified water in each bag. This will make the treatment more economical.)

3. Take off your shoes and socks and sit on the edge of the bathtub with your feet in the tub. (Or, sit on the bathroom counter with your feet in the sink—if you're agile enough.) You could also use a portable basin, if you have an assistant to help you. The basin should be large enough so that both feet can lie flat in it.

4. Wash your feet, then put each in a bag with the Noni.

5. Gently massage each foot through the plastic. Besides feeling good on your feet, the massage will help distribute the Noni evenly around them.

6. Add hot water (as hot as is bearable), to the tub in three stages.

   1. First add about an inch of hot water to the tub. This should cover your toes.

   2. Wait until the bath water cools, then add another inch of water. The water level should now cover your entire foot.

   3. When the bath water cools once again, add a few more inches of hot water to cover your ankle.

- Cover your entire foot with hot water, even if you are treating only your toes. Your toes will benefit from the increased blood circulation, which the Noni and the hot water help stimulate in your foot and ankle.

- Periodically, wiggle your toes. Stretch your feet side to side and flex them up and down. You could also massage your feet, through the plastic, while they are under water. This will increase circulation to your feet, which will enhance the Foot Bath's effects.

7. When this bath water cools, remove your feet from the plastic bags. Put your feet in the bath water to rinse off the Noni.

8. Dry your feet and apply a favorite moisturizer.

MORE ABOUT THE
NONI FOOT BATH:

Perform the Noni Foot Bath daily until your foot condition improves. Skin problems and acute foot conditions will likely improve more quickly than structural and chronic conditions. These conditions may require a daily Noni Foot Bath for several weeks before significant improvement occurs.

Do not use the Noni Foot Bath if heat is contra-indicated for your foot condition.

Step 2 (on previous page) lists minimum amounts of Noni

to use for the Foot Bath. Feel free to double these amounts for a stronger effect.

As the water level in the tub rises, the water pressure against the plastic bag will compress the bag against your foot. As a result, the Noni will be distributed all around your foot. However, if the plastic bag has a hole in it, the plastic won't cling to your foot as the water level rises. A hole will also enable water to seep into the bag. If only a few ounces of water get in, that's okay. You need not empty out the Noni and start over. But next time, use a stronger bag, or check the bag for leaks before you begin.

To help pass the time it takes to do this treatment, bring a book to read or something else to do while your feet are soaking.

When you are finished with the Noni Foot Bath, throw out the Noni fruit juice that you have used. Do not drink it or apply it elsewhere on your body. The Noni may have absorbed toxins from your foot, and your foot may have absorbed most of the Noni's healing compounds.

After the Noni Foot Bath, your feet will be red from the heat. You may notice that dry skin and calluses rub off more easily after soaking in Noni rather than in plain water. Your feet may also feel more soft and smooth.

The Noni Foot Bath will take longer to do in a bathtub than in the sink or a basin, as the larger volume of water will take longer to cool off.

The water is heated in three stages to help regulate the release of toxins from the foot, and to encourage these released toxins to move out through the bottom of the foot.

THE NONI
FOOT BATH 2

An easier alternative to the Noni Foot Bath 1.

TRY THE NONI FOOT BATH 2 FOR:

- Arthritis.
- Athlete's foot.
- Blisters.
- Bone spurs.
- Bunions.
- Calluses.
- Dry skin.
- Sore feet.

HOW TO DO
THE NONI FOOT BATH 2:

1. Before you go to bed for the night, gather the following:

    • Noni fruit juice, and a tablespoon for measuring.

    • Two large plastic bags (each big enough to cover one of your feet).

    • An old towel.

    • Adhesive tape, such as masking tape or transparent tape.

    • A pair of old thick socks.

    • Scissors.

2. Pour one-half ounce (one tablespoonful) of Noni into each bag. Return the Noni to the refrigerator and bring the other items to your bedside.

3. Lay the towel on the bed beneath the covers where your feet usually rest. The towel will prevent any Noni that may leak out from staining the linens. Get into bed.

4. Insert one foot into a plastic bag. Press the bag against your foot to release as much air from it as possible. Doing so should also spread the Noni around your foot.

5. Wrap the tape around your instep, and also around your ankle. This will secure the bag to your foot. The tape should be comfortably snug, but not so tight that it cuts off circulation.

6. Repeat Steps 4 and 5 with the other foot.

7. Massage your feet through the plastic for a few minutes each. This will also help distribute the Noni around your feet.

8. In the morning, remove the plastic bags by cutting through the tape with the scissors. Do this in the bathtub or shower where you can immediately rinse off your feet. You can even climb up onto the counter and wash your feet in the sink—if you are nimble enough. Then throw the plastic bags into the trash.

During the night, if you have to get up for some reason, put on the socks. This will ensure that the Noni will not stain your carpet in case a plastic bag breaks. Wearing the socks all night long may be too uncomfortable, though it is an option.

MORE ABOUT
THE NONI FOOT BATH 2:

This method for using Noni fruit juice on the feet is more convenient than the Noni Foot Bath 1 (page 195). Surprisingly, it is not uncomfortable to wear plastic bags on your feet all night long. This may be because the Noni feels so soothing and healing on your feet.

Although your feet will not benefit from the heat used in the Foot Bath 1, they will be exposed to Noni for a much longer period of time. Since heat helps Noni healing compounds to penetrate the body, the Foot Bath 2 may be more appropriate for conditions on the surface of the foot. However, you could put a heating pad between your feet while you rest in bed. If you use a heating pad, you would only need to do the Foot Bath 2 for an hour or two.

The instructions on the previous page suggest using one-half ounce of Noni per foot, which should be sufficient for relatively mild conditions. For more serious conditions, including pain, use as much as one ounce of Noni per foot. When using one-half ounce of Noni, it is unlikely that any Noni will leak out of the plastic bags during the night. However, leakage is more likely to occur with one ounce of liquid per bag.

You should notice some difference in the way your feet feel after only one treatment. Your skin and calluses will feel softer and your feet themselves may feel more "alive" than ever before.

The Noni Foot Bath 2 should be repeated nightly for several days for more lasting effects.

Some people may find that their feet begin to itch while performing this therapy. Unless your skin is sensitive to plastic, the itchy feeling may indicate toxins are being released from your feet.

Try massaging your feet for a few minutes, to help the toxins out. If the itchy feeling persists and becomes too uncomfortable, end the therapy. However, do try it again soon, because a release of toxins certainly indicates the technique is working.

50.

THE NONI
HAND TREATMENT 1

This treatment is as relaxing as it is effective.

TRY THE NONI
HAND TREATMENT FOR:

Various conditions of the hand including:

- Arthritis.
- Fibromyalgia.
- Injuries to the hand.
- Neuralgia.
- Skin conditions.
- Sprains.

203

HOW TO APPLY THE
NONI HAND TREATMENT:

1. Cut a piece of cheesecloth into a rectangle measuring about eight inches by about twenty inches. This size cheesecloth should be large enough to wrap completely around your hand twice. (Before you cut the cheesecloth, check to see if the suggested size fits.)

2. Pour an ounce of Noni fruit juice onto a dinner plate. Spread it around the plate with your finger. You may need more than one ounce of Noni, depending on how thick your cheesecloth is.

3. Fold the cheesecloth in half so that it now looks more like a square. Place the folded cloth on the dinner plate. Press it into the Noni to help it soak up all the juice and pulp.

4. Turn the cloth over so the pulpy side of the cloth is now facing up. Place your palm on the pulpy cloth beside the folded edge. Lift the top layer only, off the opposite edge and lay it over your hand. Your hand should now be wrapped in one layer of cheesecloth.

5. Lift your hand off the plate. Wrap the rest of the cheesecloth loosely and comfortably around your hand. Your hand should now be wrapped twice in the Noni-soaked cheesecloth.

6. Insert your wrapped hand into a plastic bag. A small sandwich bag will fit most people. Keep the bag open, to allow air to circulate around your hand. The bag should help keep your hand moist and warm, without being uncomfortable.

MORE ABOUT THE
NONI HAND TREATMENT:

Wear the Noni Hand Treatment for a couple of hours or overnight.

The Noni may get thick and sticky as it dries. It washes off easily under running water after you remove the bag and cheesecloth.

Unless someone helps you apply this treatment to both hands, you will have to treat one hand at a time.

51.

THE NONI
HAND TREATMENT 2

An easier version of an effective technique.

TRY THE NONI HAND TREATMENT 2 FOR
VARIOUS CONDITIONS OF THE HAND INCLUDING:

- Arthritis.
- Fibromyalgia.
- Injuries.
- Neuralgia.
- Skin conditions.
- Sprains.
- Stiffness.

How to do
The Noni Hand Treatment 2:

1. Refer to page 154 to make a recipe of Noni Poultice Paste, starting with one ounce of Noni fruit juice.

2. Spread the Noni Paste on one hand. Focus the Noni Paste over areas of pain and stiffness. The Paste does not have to cover the hand. Ideally, use the entire batch. But if the treatment area is small and you have some Noni Paste left over, cover it and refrigerate it for later use.

3. Place the Noni-covered hand in a plastic bag. Gently press the plastic against your hand to remove as much air from the bag as possible. Doing so will enable you to use your hands and fingers through the plastic. Gather the excess plastic that is around your wrist and twist the plastic into a few-inch long "rope," like you might twist closed a bag of chips. This will tighten the plastic around your wrist. Tuck the twisted plastic "rope" between the plastic bag and your wrist in order to secure the bag onto your hand.

4. Try this therapy at night before bed and remove the plastic in the morning. Or do the therapy while reading or watching television. Keep the pulp on for no less than an hour. Then remove the plastic and rinse your hands in water.

5. Repeat the treatment on your other hand.

More about
The Noni Hand Treatment 2:

To spread the Noni Paste on your hand, use your fingers, a spoon, or a butter spreader.

It is suggested to treat one hand at a time for practical reasons. With one hand free, you can still take part in household activities. It would also be challenging to treat both hands at the same time unless you had someone help you secure the plastic bag to the second hand.

If the treatment area is small, you could use a piece of plastic wrap instead of the plastic bag. Covering the Noni Paste with plastic simply ensures that the Noni won't rub off and stain your clothes or furniture.

I have been asked the purpose of using cheesecloth in the Noni Hand Treatment 1. Why not simply put your hand in a bag of Noni fruit juice, as suggested in the Foot Bath 2? Because the cheesecloth keeps the Noni pulp in place. If you put your hand in a plastic bag with Noni fruit juice, you would find that the juice swishes around the bag. Since a hand tends to move more than a resting foot, the Noni would not stay in one place. Therefore the concentration of Noni over any one area of the hand would constantly change. This would significantly reduce the effectiveness of the Hand Treatment. The other drawback of simply placing your hand in a bag with Noni is that the watery juice would make your fingertips feel wrinkly, which is an unpleasant feeling. If a technique is uncomfortable, people will unlikely try it a second time.

The Noni Hand Treatment 2 is easier than the Hand Treatment 1, in that you do not have to use the cheesecloth. The Noni Paste stays where you put it. The concentration of Noni healing compounds remains constant, thus maximizing the effectiveness of this technique.

After one treatment you should notice a difference in the way your hands feel, both in their flexibility and their softness. Repeat this treatment daily for several days for more lasting effects.

52.

THE NONI HEADACHE COMPRESS

Headaches come in all shapes and sizes. It has been my experience that Noni is more helpful for some kinds of headaches than for others.

TRY THIS COMPRESS FOR HEADACHES THAT ARE:

- In the front of the head.
- Focused in the temples.
- The result of eyestrain.

209

HOW TO MAKE AND APPLY THE
NONI HEADACHE COMPRESS:

1. You will need two compress pads for this procedure. The pads should be about two inches wide, and long enough to reach across your forehead, from ear to ear. You can make these pads using gauze bandage, paper towels, or an old cotton T-shirt cut to size. (Cotton absorbs moisture better than a cotton-polyester blend, of which many T-shirts are made.)

2. Pour a tablespoonful of Noni fruit juice into a bowl. Press one of the two compress pads into the juice until the pad has soaked up all the liquid. Use the pulpy side of the pad to wipe up any leftover Noni pulp that remains in the bowl.

3. Put the Noni-soaked compress pad back in the bowl, and store in the refrigerator. Cold compresses offer an analgesic effect in addition to that of Noni.

4. Pour a second tablespoonful of Noni into another bowl. Wet the second compress pad as you did the first one in Step 2 above.

5. Put the compress pad back in the bowl and bring it with you to a comfortable place where you can lie down. Put your head on a towel, which will catch any Noni fruit juice that might drip out of the Headache Compress. You may need a blanket, as the cold Compress can make your entire body feel chilled.

6. Center the pad over your forehead and lay the ends of the pad over your temples. The pulpy side of the pad should be next to your skin.

7. When the Headache Compress warms, put it in the refrigerator. Remove the one that you had previously stored there. Repeat Step 6.

8. As each Compress gets warm, use the other one. When the Compresses dry out, soak them in more Noni.

More about the
Noni Headache Compress:

If refrigerated compress pads are uncomfortably cold, keep both compress pads at room temperature. If it is too hard on your headache to make frequent trips to the refrigerator and back, lay the second compress pad over a bowl of ice that is covered with plastic. Keep the extra Compress beside you on the bed.

If Noni leaks out of the Compress, try massaging it into your scalp. This may also help your headache.

If you are on the go, or don't have time to do a Headache Compress, try rubbing some Noni seed oil on your temples, forehead, or sinuses. Noni seed oil can be obtained from your suppliers of Noni fruit juice.

In addition to the Headache Compress, consider taking a Trauma Dose (page 85). Also try the Noni Eye Poultice, to help ease light sensitivity due to the headache. You can do both the Eye Poultice and Headache Compress at the same time. If your headache stems from a neck spasm, try a Noni Poultice (page 147) over the neck, and cover it with hot towels. Also try the Noni–clay technique for headaches, on page 162. If your headaches are chronic, consider using the Procedure for Chronic Conditions, described on pages 57-59.

53.

NONI
HEMORRHOID
TREATMENTS

Relief for an embarrassing discomfort.

TRY THESE TREATMENTS FOR:

- Hemorrhoids.
- And other conditions including burning, itching and irritated anal tissue.

213

HOW TO DO THE NONI
HEMORRHOID TREATMENT METHOD 1:

1. Before bedtime, pour one teaspoonful of Noni fruit juice into a small bowl or medicine cup.

2. Press a cotton ball into the Noni until it soaks up all the Noni. Take the bowl with you into the bedroom.

3. Spread an old towel on the mid-portion of your bed's fitted sheet to protect it from being stained by the Noni.

4. Get into bed and lie down on your side.

5. Position the Noni-soaked cotton on the affected area. The pulpy side of the cotton ball should be against your skin. Press the cotton ball into your body, or against it, as needed.

6. Keep the cotton ball in place while you sleep.

HOW TO DO THE NONI
HEMORRHOID TREATMENT METHOD 2:

1. Pour one teaspoonful of Noni fruit juice into a small bowl or medicine cup.

2. Press a cotton ball into the Noni until it soaks up all the Noni. Take the bowl with you into the bathroom.

3. Adhere a sanitary napkin to your underwear.

4. Sit on the toilet. Position the Noni-soaked cotton on the affected area. The pulpy side of the cotton ball should be against your skin. Press the cotton ball into your body, or against it, as needed.

5. Stand up carefully so that the cotton ball stays put. Replace your underwear. The sanitary napkin will protect your clothing from any Noni that may leak out. Go about your day, enjoying the relief that Noni can provide.

Perform either or both of the above Methods as often as needed.

MORE ABOUT THE
NONI HEMORRHOID TREATMENTS:

You should expect some relief on the first application. However constant contact between Noni and the affected area may be required to achieve and maintain comfort. This may mean repeating Method 2 every few minutes, and then gradually less often.

Men may object to the sanitary napkin. They may be able to omit that step if they put less Noni in the cotton ball. Then the Noni will be less likely to drip.

A cotton ball made of pure cotton is preferable to "cosmetic puffs," which look like cotton balls but are made of synthetic fiber. Cotton holds more Noni than synthetic fiber. It also tends to adhere better to the skin.

Soaking the cotton ball in refrigerated Noni fruit juice makes the cotton ball like a miniature cold-pack, which has its own pain-relieving properties.

NONI MASSAGE

A Noni massage is a real treat!

TRY A NONI MASSAGE FOR:

- Sore muscles.
- Low vitality.
- Illness.
- Nerve and muscle pain.
- When the body seems to radiate stress.

HOW TO MAKE
NONI MASSAGE OIL:

1. Pour some of your favorite unscented massage oil into a container such as a bowl, cup, or plastic oil bottle. (Sesame oil or another lightweight oil is particularly nice.)

2. Estimate how much oil you have. Add no more than an equal amount of Noni fruit juice. Any more than this can make the Noni-oil combination too pulpy and sticky.

3. Mix the oil and juice together with your finger. Or, if you have added the oil and juice to a bottle, shake the bottle. Shaking will produce the best emulsion.

4. Test the consistency, and add more oil or Noni as needed.

5. Apply the Noni Massage Oil as you would any massage oil.

MORE ABOUT
NONI MASSAGE:

The Noni and oil combination separates quickly. Remix it each time before you apply more to the body.

If you plan to use up the mixture within a few days, it need not be refrigerated.

Expect muscle tension and stress to be relieved more quickly when incorporating Noni fruit juice into a massage. Noni Massage Oil can also have a therapeutic effect on skin conditions and makes the skin feel wonderfully soft.

A massage therapist's hands will also appreciate the Noni Massage Oil, not only because of the skin-softening effect, but also because they won't tire as quickly.

Enhance the benefits of Noni Massage by offering the person who will receive the massage, an ounce of Noni to drink before the massage begins. Drinking Noni enhances the beneficial effects of Noni applied topically.

55.

THE NONI
NAIL TREATMENT

This procedure may be done on a single nail, all the finger-nails, or the toenails.

USE THE NONI
NAIL TREATMENT FOR:

- Brittle and broken nails.
- Ingrown toenails.
- Nail fungus.
- Nail infections.
- Unhealthy cuticles.
- Unhealthy nails.

How to Apply the
Noni Nail Treatment:

1. Pour one or two teaspoonfuls of Noni into a bowl.

2. Tear a cotton ball into pieces large enough to cover each of the nails you want to treat.

   Optional: massage each nail by squeezing it several times between your thumb and forefinger. This will improve circulation to the nail, and enhance the benefits of the Noni Nail therapy.

3. Dip one side of a cotton piece into the Noni fruit juice. It should be only half wet. The dry part will soak up the excess juice, so it won't drip.

4. Place the Noni side of the cotton on the nail to cover it. Press gently to help adhere the wet cotton to your nail.

5. Repeat Steps 3 and 4 for the other nails you want to treat.

More about the
Noni Nail Treatment:

Keep the Noni Nail Treatment in place for at least an hour, or overnight if you do the treatment right before bedtime. For general nail care, do the Nail Treatment once every week or two, or every time you cut your nails.

If you have just used nail polish remover, wash your hands well with soap before applying the Nail Treatment.

If a nail problem is serious or painful, do the Noni Nail Treatment daily.

If the Nail Treatment is applied often, your nails should grow stronger and more healthy.

If you do this treatment while you are resting, the surface tension of the wet cotton may be enough to keep the cotton pieces in place. But if you want to move around, secure the cotton to your nail with first-aid paper tape.

56.

THE NONI
RASH PLASTER

The Noni Rash Plaster is used specifically for skin conditions.

TRY A RASH PLASTER
FOR CONDITIONS INCLUDING:

- Burns.
- Chicken pox.
- Diaper rash.
- Eczema.
- Hives.
- Liver spots.

- Poison Ivy.
- Psoriasis.
- Scars.
- Skin eruptions.
- Stretch marks.
- Pimples and acne.

How to Make and Apply
A Noni Rash Plaster:

1. Select a plaster cloth that will cover the area you want to treat. You may use cheesecloth, an unfolded sterile gauze pad, a piece of an old T-shirt, or a paper towel. A plaster cloth should be thinner than a pad used for compresses or poultices.

2. Pour some Noni fruit juice into a bowl. The amount of Noni you will need depends on the size of the plaster cloth you are using. Start with one-half tablespoonful of Noni, and add more if needed.

   If your plaster cloth is bigger than four inches square, pour the Noni onto a dinner plate. This will make it easier to distribute the Noni evenly throughout the plaster cloth.

3. Press the plaster cloth into the juice. Do not turn the cloth over.

4. Hold the cloth over the bowl and squeeze the cloth gently so excess juice can drip off. The cloth should be wet, but not dripping wet.

5. Lay the plaster cloth over the treatment area to cover it. The pulpy side of the cloth should be touching the skin. The plaster will feel cold at first, but will soon warm up with body heat.

6. Press the plaster cloth onto the skin and mold it around the contours of your body. The plaster cloth will be slightly adhesive; perhaps just enough that you won't need to secure it in place. If you do need to secure it, don't use plastic. In this case, you want the area to breathe—the skin heals better that way. Try wrapping the plaster cloth with gauze bandage instead.

   Apply additional plaster cloths as needed to completely cover all the skin to be treated. The Noni Rash Plaster can cover a considerably large portion of the body if necessary.

7. Leave the plaster cloth in place until it dries. Then rinse out the cloth, soak it in more Noni, and reapply.

More about the
Noni Rash Plaster:

Apply the Noni Rash Plaster as often as needed.

In cases of contagious rashes, such as Poison Ivy, you may leave the Rash Plaster in place even when it dries out. This may prevent the rash from spreading. But keeping the plaster wet with Noni may help control the itching.

Think twice before using the Noni Rash Plaster for pimples or acne on the face. Noni fruit juice can stain open skin a purple color.

For diaper rash, apply the Noni Rash Plaster on the reddened area. Then put on the diaper. The diaper will hold the Plaster in place. When you change the diaper, throw out the plaster cloth. Then reapply the Rash Plaster using a clean plaster cloth soaked in more Noni. My babies' diaper rashes have cleared up remarkably quickly using this technique.

To warm the Rash Plaster before placing it on your baby's bottom, prepare the Plaster as in Steps 1 through 3, but use a glass bowl. Add a few inches of very hot tap water to the bathroom sink. Place the bowl, which contains the Noni-soaked Rash Plaster, in the hot water to warm. Be sure none of the water gets into the bowl. In the meantime, clean up the baby. By the time you are ready to apply the Noni Rash Plaster, the plaster cloth should be warm. Test its temperature before you place it on the baby.

57.

THE NONI SCALP TREATMENT

Don't worry, this treatment will not turn your hair purple!

TRY THE NONI SCALP TREATMENT FOR:

Various scalp conditions including:

- Dandruff.
- Eczema.
- Psoriasis.
- Itchy scalp.
- Scalp sores.

How to Apply the
Noni Scalp Treatment:

1. Pour some Noni fruit juice in a medicine cup or small plastic cup. You will need at least one tablespoonful. Use as much as two ounces if your condition is throughout your scalp, if you have a lot of hair, or if your condition is relatively severe.

2. Wrap a towel around your neck and shoulders.

3. Hold the cup with the Noni over your head. Part the hair over a section of your scalp. Pour some of the juice on this area so the Noni makes direct contact with your skin. As you pour the juice on, massage it into your hair so it does not drip off your head.

4. Repeat Step 3 with different sections of your scalp. Apply the Noni to your entire scalp, or just those areas that need it. Put a second and third coat of juice over problem areas.

5. When you have applied all the Noni, massage it into your scalp for a few minutes.

6. Brush or comb your hair. Then let it air dry, or cover your head with a towel or an old shower-cap.

7. Keep the Noni on for a few hours, or overnight, or just until it dries. Then rinse out the Noni fruit juice and wash your hair.

More about the
Noni Scalp Treatment:

Repeat this procedure daily until the condition improves.

You may need someone else's help to do this procedure, especially if you find it difficult to reach your arms up over your head.

If you have little or no hair, the Noni Rash Plaster (page 221), may work better for you.

Besides having a therapeutic effect on scalp conditions, the Noni Scalp Treatment may also help to alleviate headaches.

If you do this treatment before bed, cover your pillowcase with a towel to prevent the juice from staining it.

Noni fruit juice applied to your scalp acts somewhat like styling gel—with a fruity fragrance.

In researching whether Noni can be used safely on the hair, I collected many hair samples that included natural, treated, as well as gray hair. Part of each sample was soaked in Noni fruit juice for over twenty-four hours, and then studied. I also examined the samples under a microscope.

Noni appeared to have no negative effect on the natural and gray hair samples. I noticed that after using Noni on my own scalp (I kept it there until it dried, and then washed it off), my natural hair seemed softer and to have more "body."

The effects of Noni on treated hair varied and were inconclusive. This is not surprising, since there are so many different kinds of hair treatments. Just to be safe, those who have treated hair and wish to do the Noni Scalp Treatment, should wash off the Noni after about twenty to thirty minutes. This is plenty of time to allow the Noni to work on your scalp, while not interfering with your hair treatment.

58.

THE NONI SITZ BATH

A bath of Noni fruit juice? Well, not exactly.

TRY THE NONI SITZ BATH FOR:

- Childbirth recovery.
- Conditions of the anus.
- Conditions of the bladder and urethra.
- Conditions of the male genital organs.
- Conditions of the vagina and labia.
- Hemorrhoids.
- Hernias.
- Menstrual cramps.

How to Take
A Noni Sitz Bath:

1. Fill the bathtub with three inches of hot water. Use water that is hotter than you would normally add to a bathtub.

2. Pour three ounces of Noni fruit juice into the bath water.

3. Step into the water. Sit down slowly to give yourself time to acclimate to the hot water. When you are seated, keep your knees bent so that the only parts of your body in the water are your feet and bottom.

4. Rest in the tub for at least fifteen minutes or until the water cools. Every so often, move your hands through the water to keep the Noni pulp well mixed throughout the bath water. The Noni water will be very soothing to your bottom.

More about
The Noni Sitz Bath:

If you think you may get chilly while sitting in a tub with relatively little water, wear an old t-shirt or wrap yourself with a towel that you don't mind getting wet.

You can also add other herbs or herbal teas to the bath water that are appropriate for your condition.

Bending your knees so that your feet are also in the water is therapeutic for two reasons. First, the feet have points and meridians that connect to every organ and area of the body. The heated Noni-water will indirectly stimulate the entire body through these points. Second, having your feet in the hot Noni-water will draw energy down your body. Too much energy often gets stuck in our head, especially if we have to think a lot at work, or if we tend to get caught in thoughts or other mental habits such as worry, impatience, or being chronically upset. When energy gets caught in the head, then the body has difficulty moving it to areas that need it to heal. When our feet are stimulated, as they are in this therapy, this energy is given a pathway to move downward. The body can then direct this energy wherever it is needed most. You can choose where the body will direct this energy by stimulating that area in some way. In this case, that other area is also submerged in the hot Noni-water bath.

When the bath is over, you will not need to rinse yourself off before getting out. The Noni pulp is well-enough spread throughout the bath water that it does not coat your body. Any Noni residue will be minimal and may also be mildly therapeutic.

THE NONI SMALL AREA TREATMENT

This is also called a "Mini-compress."

USE THE NONI SMALL AREA TREATMENT FOR:

- Bee stings.
- Boils and abscesses.
- Infected pierced earring holes.
- Insect and spider bites.
- Moles.
- Puncture wounds.
- Single pimples or acne.

- Small bruises.
- Small scars.
- Warts.

233

HOW TO MAKE AND APPLY
THE NONI SMALL AREA TREATMENT:

1. Tear off a one-half inch piece of a cotton ball. Shape this cotton piece so it is somewhat round. If the target area is a relatively large abscess, bruise or scar, you may need to use a whole cotton ball. Also use a whole cotton ball if the target area is painful.

2. Dip the cotton in Noni fruit juice, so half of it is wet.

3. Place the wet side of the cotton over the target area.

4. The surface tension of the wet cotton may be enough to keep the cotton attached to your skin, even if you move around. If the target area is underneath clothing, or if you are particularly active, you may secure the cotton with first-aid tape or with an adhesive bandage.

MORE ABOUT THE NONI
SMALL AREA TREATMENT:

Most conditions for which this Mini-compress is applied clear up more quickly if you use the pulpier part of the Noni fruit juice. So be sure to gently shake the Noni bottle before pouring Noni to treat small areas.

Wet only half the cotton ball so that the dry portion can soak up excess liquid. This will prevent the Mini-compress from leaking.

Some moles, warts, and small scars may require daily application for a few weeks before you notice significant changes. Try applying the Noni Small Area Treatment on these areas every night before bed. Acute problems may require only a few applications.

60.

The Noni
Topical Splash

The Topical Splash is helpful for skin conditions that cover relatively large areas, or when you need quick relief when on the go.

Use a Noni Topical Splash for:

- Allergic reactions.
- Burns.
- Chicken pox.
- Eczema.
- Pimples and acne.
- Poison ivy.
- Psoriasis.

- Rashes.
- Skin irritations.
- Sunburn.

How to Apply a
Noni Topical Splash:

1. Pour an ounce of Noni fruit juice into a small glass bowl or container.

2. Measure three tablespoonfuls (one-and-a-half ounces) of purified water. Pour the water into the Noni in a slow, steady, uninterrupted stream. Meanwhile, swirl the bottle for several seconds to mix the liquids together.

3. Apply the Noni-water mixture to the skin with a cotton ball, or splash it on with the palm of your hand. Then gently rub the Noni around the area with your hand.

4. When the liquid dries (usually no more than a minute), apply the Noni a second time and possibly a third time.

5. Use the Topical Splash as often during the day as you like. Repeat the Splash daily as needed.

More about the
Noni Topical Splash:

Don't shake the Noni bottle before pouring. Skin conditions respond better to the watery part of the Noni fruit juice, found at the top of a new bottle of Noni (which has been left undisturbed). Using the pulpy part of the juice can leave pulp remnants on the skin. This is not a bad thing, but it can look unsightly.

Noni by itself can feel sticky when applied to the skin. Adding one-and-a-half parts of purified water dilutes the Noni just enough to keep it effective, without becoming sticky. Nor will this ratio of Noni and water give the skin a purple cast.

The Topical Splash can leave the skin feeling soft and smooth. It can also reduce itchiness and irritation on contact.

Store the Topical Splash in a small glass jar. A tincture bottle, with an eyedropper for a lid, is even better. You can carry it with you, and whenever you need to, use the eyedropper to place a few drops of the Noni-water mixture on your skin. Then gently spread the Noni over the affected area with your fingertips. Keep the Topical Splash in the refrigerator when you are not carrying it with you.

The Noni Tummy Treatment 1

The Noni Tummy Treatment is used on the lower abdomen, on and below the bellybutton.

Use the Noni Tummy Treatment 1 When:

- A child is ill.
- A child refuses to drink Noni.
- An individual is in a coma or has lost consciousness and you and a medical team have done everything else you can do.
- Drinking Noni causes nausea.

    (cont.)

- Drinking Noni causes a cleansing reaction which is too strong.
- You are unable to take liquids orally.
- You want to benefit from Noni, but are allergic to it or are hypersensitive to its effects.
- You want to support the body through a fever.

The Noni Tummy
Treatment 1 is also Helpful for:

- Conditions of the intestine and abdomen.
- Endometriosis.
- Heavy metal or chemical toxicity.
- Systemic candida.
- Intestinal parasite infestation.

How to Apply a
Noni Tummy Treatment 1:

1. Select a compress pad:
   - Use a 2" x 2" gauze pad for infants and a 4" x 4" gauze pad for babies.
   - For children, teens, and adults who have somewhat flat tummies, use a paper napkin for the compress pad. Paper napkins are about six inches square, and large enough to cover the required area.
   - Adults with larger tummies can use a compress pad made of a facecloth, or three paper towels laid one on top of the other, like a sandwich.
2. Heat a glass bowl by pouring very hot tap water or heated water into it. After several seconds, when the bowl is hot, pour out the water and quickly dry the bowl.
3. Pour the amount of Noni fruit juice that you will need into the heated bowl. (See the information box on page 146

for an idea of how much liquid you may need.)

4. Place the compress pad on the Noni fruit juice, and gently press down on the pad to help it soak up all the liquid. When you remove the pad from the bowl, wipe up any pulp that remains in the bowl with the pulpy side of the pad.

5. Place the wet pad over the lower abdomen, such that the top inch of the pad completely covers the bellybutton. People who are overweight should center the Tummy Treatment over the bellybutton. The pulpy side of the pad should be touching the skin.

6. Cover the compress pad with plastic wrap, and then with an old hand-towel.

MORE ABOUT THE
NONI TUMMY TREATMENT 1:

A Noni Tummy Treatment may be made with Noni alone, or with equal parts of Noni and purified water.

- It is easier, and preferable, to use undiluted Noni when applying the Tummy Treatment on babies and children.

- Adults who are using a facecloth or paper towels for a compress pad may need two or three ounces or more of Noni. If they would prefer a more economical application, they may dilute the Noni with an equal amount of purified water. Diluting the Noni with this proportion of water may actually help the Noni healing compounds reach into the adult body.

If you are adding water:

1. Measure the amount of Noni you will need and pour it into the heated bowl.

2. Measure an equal amount of purified water and add this to the Noni in a slow, steady, uninterrupted stream.

3. Swirl the two liquids together, or stir them briefly with your finger. Then wet the poultice pad.

Keep the Tummy Treatment in place for at least a few hours. Apply it once or twice a day, or as often as needed until the condition improves.

People who prefer to sleep on their back could apply the Tummy Treatment at night, just before going to bed.

If the compress pad cools off by the time you are ready to apply it to the body, leave the pad in the bowl of Noni. Then place the bottom half of the bowl in a container or sink full of hot water. Apply the compress pad when it is warmed enough for you.

For babies who are ill, give the Tummy Treatment each time you do a diaper change. A gauze pad can completely cover their lower tummies. The diaper will hold the Tummy Treatment in place, so you won't need plastic wrap for that purpose. Besides, the plastic might irritate their delicate skin. However, you may use a piece of plastic folded to the same size as the compress pad to cover the Tummy Treatment. This will prevent the diaper from soaking up the Noni. The diaper will protect the clothing from being stained, but you may need a larger sized diaper than usual.

Adults could hold the Tummy Treatment in place by wearing it inside a pair of pants. Select a pair that you don't mind getting stained—in case some Noni fruit juice leaks out. This method allows you to move around, without anyone knowing that you are wearing a compress pad.

There are two ways to place the compress pad on the body.

1. Have the upper edge perpendicular to the body's midline (the imaginary line that runs down the center of the body, dividing its right and left sides). This edge should overlap the bellybutton by about an inch.

2. Place the pad diagonally on the body, with the upper corner of the pad covering the bellybutton.

Tummy Treatments (both 1 and 2) are the next best thing to drinking Noni for two reasons. First, Noni's healing compounds enter the body through the bellybutton more quickly than through skin elsewhere on the body (except under the tongue). Second, the Noni healing compounds that enter the body through the bellybutton tend to remain in the abdominal area and work there, rather than spreading throughout the body as they do when taken orally.

41.

THE NONI TUMMY
TREATMENT 2

So that's what bellybuttons are for!

TRY THE NONI
TUMMY TREATMENT 2 FOR:

Conditions of the abdomen including:

- Abdominal pain (be sure to also consult a medical professional).
- Bloating.
- Constipation.
- Diarrhea.
- Fever.
- Indigestion.
    (cont.)

243

• Parasite and yeast infestation.

And as an alternative way to get Noni's healing compounds into infants and children.

How to do The Noni Tummy Treatment 2:

1. Hold a teacup under very hot tap water to warm the cup. When it is hot, quickly dry the cup with a towel.

2. Pour about one or two teaspoonfuls of Noni fruit juice into the hot teacup. This will warm the juice.

3. Press a cotton ball into the Noni. The cotton ball should be saturated with Noni, and may be dripping wet.

4. Bring the teacup with the cotton ball and Noni to a comfortable location where you can lie down for a while.

5. Lie on your back, and insert the Noni-soaked cotton ball into your bellybutton.

More about The Noni Tummy Treatment 2:

The cotton ball should be large enough to completely fill and cover the bellybutton. Use half a cotton ball for youngsters.

Be sure to check the temperature of the Noni before you place it on a child's body—or your own, for that matter.

If you perform this treatment while taking a nap or before going to bed at night, place an old towel beneath you to protect the bed linens from being stained in case the cotton ball falls out.

Keep the cotton ball in place for at least fifteen minutes, and longer if possible. If treating infants, a diaper can secure the cotton ball in place. First aid tape could be used on older children and adults. Be prepared to wipe up any Noni that drips out when you stand up.

Older children, teens, and many adults may prefer the Tummy Treatment 1 because having a Noni soaked compress pad on your stomach can feel very soothing. But, the Tummy

Treatment 2 is easier to apply. The Tummy Treatment 2 would also work better for overweight teens and adults, and for children who won't lie still long enough to keep a compress pad in place. The oddity of putting a Noni-soaked cotton ball in their bellybuttons can intrigue children enough that they will allow you to do it.

SECTION 3

OTHER INTERNAL
APPLICATIONS OF NONI

Drinking Noni and applying it topically are the two most obvious uses of Noni. But this remarkable juice can also be therapeutic in ways that one might not expect. If it seems too odd to try putting fruit juice in your nose or ears, for example, don't think of Noni as a juice drink. Think of it as the liquid extract of an amazing tropical fruit, which contains special healing compounds.

This Section describes procedures for many internal applications of Noni fruit juice. The applications are listed alphabetically.

When you use internal applications, plan to drink Noni as well. Oral and internal Noni applications will enhance each other's benefits. To decide how much Noni fruit juice to take orally, select a procedure in Section 1 that best suits your condition. Internal applications also draw the healing compounds from the Noni that you drink to those parts of the body where the Noni is applied.

63.

THE NONI ANTI-ACID SUBSTITUTE

Though Noni does not work in the same way as regular anti-acids, the end results are often just as relieving.

TRY THE NONI
ANTI-ACID SUBSTITUTE FOR:

- Heartburn.
- Indigestion.
- Stomach distress from overeating.
  (cont.)

249

- Also, if you are relatively healthy, but unaccustomed to certain foods like refined sugar, meat, or "junk" food, Noni may help your body handle these foods on those special occasions when you do eat them.

HOW TO USE NONI
AS AN ANTI-ACID SUBSTITUTE:

1. Drink one ounce of Noni following your meal, either before or after symptoms arise.
2. If you don't feel better after a few minutes, try drinking another ounce.

MORE ABOUT THE
NONI ANTI-ACID SUBSTITUTE:

The effects of taking Noni before a meal verses after it, are different. Noni taken before a meal, on an empty stomach, will help treat the underlying cause of stomach distress. Taking the Noni Anti-acid Substitute after a meal, will better address the symptoms of a stomach condition.

For chronic indigestion, try the Procedure for Chronic Conditions (page 57), which suggests taking three ounces of Noni a day. Take one of these three ounces a few minutes before each meal. Then eat mindfully. If you still feel distress afterwards, take a tablespoonful or more of Noni after the meal. Eventually, you may not need the Noni Anti-acid Substitute any more.

Taking an ounce of Noni before each meal can also help curb your appetite if you tend to overeat.

The Noni Fast Method 2 (page 107) is another approach to dealing with chronic indigestion and heartburn. If you do the Fast to help a stomach condition, try taking some of the Noni-water mixture (page 108) that is used for the Fast, both before and after each meal.

64.

The Noni Douche

Noni fruit juice may be added to a douche bag filled with water.

Use a Noni Douche
For Conditions such as:

- Menstrual cramps.
- Vaginal itching.
- Vaginal odor.
- Yeast infections.
- Personal hygiene after intercourse.

251

How to use
A Noni Douche:

1. Fill a douche bag with warm, purified water. Add one or two ounces of Noni fruit juice to the bag. Attach the tube to the bag, and attach the applicator to the tube.

2. Find a position in the shower or bathtub that is comfortable. You may stand, squat, kneel on one knee, or lie on your back—many positions will work. You could even douche over the toilet seat.

3. Hold the douche bag above your waistline. Hold the tube lower than this, and allow any air in the tube to empty out. When the Noni-water liquid starts to come out, quickly insert the applicator into your body. Insert it as far as it will go comfortably.

4. Move the applicator as necessary to allow the liquid to cleanse the entire area. The Noni-water liquid will spill out of your body as you perform the douche.

More about
The Noni Douche:

Have a sanitary pad or panty liner ready to wear when you are finished. Any juice that leaks out could stain your clothing or the bathroom carpet.

Symptoms can be alleviated seconds after douching, though sometimes it takes a few hours to feel relief. For more stubborn or serious cases, try the Noni Vaginal Implant (page 291).

For menstrual cramps and other symptoms of PMS, try the Procedure for Chronic Conditions (page 57). Do the Noni Douche daily starting two weeks before you expect menstruation to begin.

65.

NONI
EAR DROPS

Noni Ear Drops are effective for children and adults, as well as for pets. This chapter offers three methods for applying Noni Ear Drops on yourself or others, and with or without an eyedropper.

TRY NONI EAR DROPS
FOR CONDITIONS SUCH AS:

- Chronic dizzy spells.
- Ear infections.
- Ear pain.
- Headaches.

- Headaches.
- Loss of hearing.
- Impaired hearing.

HOW TO APPLY
NONI EAR DROPS
METHOD 1:

1. Fill a clean glass eyedropper with Noni fruit juice.

2. Hold the eyedropper under hot water to warm the juice.

3. Put a drop of the warmed Noni on the back of your hand to test its temperature. If the Noni is still too cold, put the dropper back under the hot water. If the Noni feels too hot, wait a minute while the air temperature cools it off, then retest.

4. Have the person who is to receive the Noni Ear Drops lie down, facing sideways on the bed. Place a towel on the pillow, as any Noni that may leak out of the ear will stain the bed linens.

5. Apply the Noni Ear Drops:

    • For children: Place two or three drops of warm Noni fruit juice inside the ear.

    • For adults: Keep adding drops until the ear canal is filled with juice.

6. With your fingertip, gently rub behind the ear and just underneath it, to work the juice towards the eardrum.

7. Pack the ear with a small piece of cotton.

8. Repeat Steps 5, 6, and 7 with the other ear.

HOW TO APPLY
NONI EAR DROPS
METHOD 2

Use this method if you don't have an eyedropper and if you are applying Noni Ear Drops into your own ears.

1. Warm about two teaspoonfuls of Noni fruit juice as described in the information box below.

2. Soak the end of a Q-tip in the warm Noni. Touch this wet end of the Q-tip against your cheek to check the Noni's temperature.

3. If you are applying the Noni Ear Drops to yourself, lie on your side and drape a towel over your neck and behind your ear. Press the wet end of the Q-tip against the opening of your ear canal. This will cause some of the Noni to drip into your ear. You may have to dip the Q-tip back in the Noni and repeat this step a few times until your ear is filled.

If you are using this method on someone else, simply hold the Q-tip over the ear canal's opening. Then squeeze the cotton tip to release the juice into the ear.

4. Use the other side of the Q-tip to wipe up any Noni on the outer ear that didn't make it into the ear canal.

5. With your fingertip, gently rub behind the ear and just underneath it, to work the juice towards the eardrum.

6. Pack the ear with a piece of cotton.

7. Repeat this procedure for the other ear, using a new Q-tip.

How to Warm Noni
Ear Drops for Methods 2 and 3

1. Heat a glass or porcelain teacup by filling it with boiling water or very hot tap water.

2. After about fifteen seconds, pour out the water. The cup should be very hot.

3. Quickly dry the cup and pour in a couple teaspoonfuls of Noni fruit juice.

4. Apply the Noni immediately, before the juice cools.

How to Apply
Noni Ear Drops
Method 3:

This method does not employ an eyedropper and is not recommended for children because of the small size of their ears.

1. Warm about two teaspoonfuls of Noni fruit juice as described in the information box on the previous page.

2. Tear apart a cotton ball to make two pieces the right size to plug the opening of each ear.

3. Dip one cotton ball into the warmed Noni fruit juice so that half of it is wet. Touch the wet cotton to your cheek to check its temperature.

4. Lie on your side and hold the wet cotton over your ear canal. The wet side of the cotton should be facing your body. Squeeze the juice into your ear.

5. Then pack the same piece of cotton gently inside your ear, with the wet side facing in.

6. With your fingertip, gently rub behind your ear and just underneath it, to work the juice towards the eardrum.

7. Repeat Steps 3 through 6 with your other ear.

More about
Noni Ear Drops:

Noni Ear Drops may be applied two or three times a day.

Before pouring Noni fruit juice for Noni Ear Drops, gently turn the Noni bottle upside-down then right side up a few times. A nice mix of the pulpier part and the watery part of the Noni makes the best Noni Ear Drops. Avoid shaking the Noni bottle so much that air bubbles form. The ear is a relatively small area. Air bubbles in the Ear Drops would prevent the Noni from reaching all of the ear.

Massage any unused Noni Ear Drops onto swollen glands, on the left and right sides of the neck.

Our family has enjoyed relief from minor ear infections after only one or two treatments. (This was verified by examining the ears with an otoscope.) Several treatments may be necessary for more serious conditions.

Chronic ear conditions may require Noni Ear Drop treatments daily for several weeks. Meanwhile, follow the Procedure for Chronic Conditions (page 57).

For acute ear conditions, also follow the Procedure for Acute Conditions (page 55).

If an ear condition is painful, apply Noni Ear Drops and then apply a Noni Compress (page 143). One way to do this is to use a thin compress pad that is about four inches square. Gently press the Noni-soaked compress pad around the ear so it conforms to the contours of the ear. Another option is to apply a small Noni-soaked cotton ball in the indentation behind the earlobe. Apply the Noni Ear Drops daily for a few days, even after the pain subsides.

If a physician examines your ears after you have put Noni Ear Drops in them, let the doctor know that you have used Noni. The ear canal may contain purple remnants of Noni pulp. Sometimes, however, there is no trace of Noni in the ear. The ear seems to have eagerly absorbed the Noni, purple and all.

66.

THE NONI ENEMA

A relatively small amount of Noni fruit juice in an enema bag can make a big difference.

TRY A NONI ENEMA
FOR CONDITIONS SUCH AS:

- Constipation.
- Detoxification.
- Heavy metal poisoning.
- Inflammation.
- Parasites.

259

HOW TO TAKE
A NONI ENEMA:

1. Add warm water to a standard, two-quart enema bag until it is nearly full. If your tap water is chlorinated, use heated purified water. Test the temperature of the water in the bag with your finger to make sure it isn't too hot.

2. Add one tablespoonful of Noni fruit juice to the enema bag. If you are taking a series of enemas, gradually increase this amount. You could use up to eight ounces (one cup) of Noni per enema bag.

3. Attach the enema tube to the bag, and the enema applicator to the tube. Lubricate the applicator with an herbal ointment. Don't use a mentholated ointment—it will sting!

4. Hold the enema bag over the sink, and allow any air trapped in the bag to exit through the tube. When Noni-water liquid starts to come out of the bag, squeeze the stopper that is attached to the tube. This will stop the flow of the liquid.

5. Hook the enema bag onto a shower door or the bathroom door handle. Place an old towel on the bathroom floor. Find a comfortable position on the floor. I prefer to lie on one side. You could also lean over on your hands and knees.

6. Insert the applicator into your body. Release the stopper that is attached to the tube. Try to relax, to allow the liquid to enter your intestines. Squeeze the stopper as needed to regulate the flow of the Noni-water liquid into your body.

7. When you feel an urge to expel the liquid, squeeze the stopper and remove the applicator from your body. Try to retain the liquid for a few minutes. If the urge passes, and if you were able to successfully retain the liquid, try massaging your lower abdomen. This will help break up any accumulation in your intestines. Massage in the direction that food usually goes when passing through the intestines—looking down at your abdomen, this would be in a clockwise circle. Insert more Noni-water when you can.

8. When you are ready, expel the enema into the toilet. Some people are able to retain the entire contents of the enema bag. Others can only retain a portion of the enema at a time.

MORE ABOUT
THE NONI ENEMA:

Noni fruit juice added to an enema can help the intestines feel soothed and peaceful, despite the relative stress of the enema itself.

If your colon is very unhealthy, think twice about filling the enema bag a second time and doing an enema immediately following the first. It may be too much activity for the intestines at one time.

Experiment with different amounts of Noni in the enema bag. This way you can find an amount that suits you best.

You may add Noni along with other natural substances that are sometimes included in enemas, such as sea-salt and liquid chlorophyll.

You may find parasites expelled into the toilet bowl, but microscopic parasites may also be eliminated, which you won't be able to see.

Here are guidelines for how often to take the Noni Enema:

- Take the enema once a day for a week.
- Then take the enema every other day for a couple of weeks.
- Gradually decrease the frequency of the enemas to once a week.
- If symptoms recur, repeat this schedule.

Adjust these suggestions to meet your personal needs.

During a detoxification crisis, Noni enemas can help calm and stabilize the body. Take a series of enemas and decrease the amount of Noni fruit juice that you use each time. For example, the first day you might start with two ounces of

Noni fruit juice in the enema bag. The second day, you might use one ounce and the third day, add only one tablespoonful.

Whereas decreasing the amount of Noni used in a series of enemas helps to slow down a cleansing reaction, increasing the amount of Noni used in each enema would intensify a detoxification.

Noni fruit juice may also be used for colonic irrigation, which is a special procedure performed by Colon Therapists. A Noni Colonic Irrigation is more thorough and effective than a Noni Enema, and reaches farther up the intestine. Add about five ounces of Noni to the colon-therapy machine (use at least two ounces, and as much as eight to ten ounces). Perform the colonic irrigation as usual. Noni fruit juice added to a colonic irrigation can help the intestines feel soothed and peaceful, despite the relative stress of the colon therapy itself.

67.

NONI EYE DROPS

Noni fruit juice may be used in the eyes. But enough water should be added to adequately disperse the Noni pulp.

USE NONI
EYE DROPS FOR:

Various conditions of the eyelid and the surface of the eye including:

- Allergic reactions that affect the eyes.
- Conjunctivitis.
- Infections.
- Inflammation.
- Itchy eyes.
- Pink-eye.
- Tear gland infections.

How to Make and
Apply Noni Eye Drops:

1. Pour a tablespoonful of Noni fruit juice in a clean cup.

2. Measure four tablespoonfuls (one-quarter cup) of purified water in a measuring cup.

3. Pour the purified water into the Noni fruit juice in a slow, steady, uninterrupted stream, while swirling the liquids together. You have now made Noni Eye Drops.

4. Hold the full eyedropper in a cup of hot tap water. This will warm the Noni-water mixture.

5. Squeeze out a drop or two of Noni Eye Drops onto the back of your hand. This serves two purposes: 1) It lets you test the temperature of the liquid. 2) It removes any tap water that might have seeped into the eyedropper while warming it.

6. Place a few drops of Noni Eye Drops in each eye.

More about
Noni Eye Drops:

Do not shake the Noni bottle before measuring juice for Noni Eye Drops. The watery portion of the juice, found at the top of a new bottle of Noni (which has been left undisturbed), is better for Eye Drops.

Noni Eye Drops can be applied several times a day.

As with other kinds of eye drops, the eyes may sting for a few seconds after administering the drops. A soothing feeling should follow. Interestingly, some people don't feel the sting at all, or feel it only sometimes.

Keep the Noni Eye Drops in the refrigerator. But make a fresh batch each day you plan to use them. At the end of the day, drink any unused Noni-water mixture that you may have leftover, so it won't be wasted. This oral dose can also be helpful for your eye condition.

Consider supplementing the Eye Drops treatment with a Noni Eye Poultice (page 177). Eye Drops are especially helpful for conditions on the surface of the eye, whereas the Eye Poultice can uplift the health of the entire eye.

For relatively serious eye conditions, also use a Procedure for Serious Conditions (pages 65 and 69). For eye conditions that are chronic, but not so serious, also use the Procedure for Chronic Conditions (page 57).

An Alternative Method
For Taking Noni Eye Drops

If you don't like taking eye drops, you may be grateful to know there is an alternative. This is the preferred method for giving Noni Eye Drops to children. It may be easier to use this method on yourself, as well.

1. Make a Noni Eye Poultice pad as described on page 178, or simply use two cotton balls.

2. Dip the poultice pad (or cotton balls) in the Noni-water mixture that you made in Steps 1 and 2 on the previous page.

3. Place the poultice pad over your eyes. The liquid may drip off your face; so put a towel under your head.

4. Gently press the poultice pad into the inside corners of your eyes and roll your eyeballs around. This will release the Noni-water mixture into your eyes in a gentle way that you can easily control.

5. Remove the poultice pad after the eyes have been bathed in Noni. Of course, if you like, you may leave the poultice pad in place for fifteen to thirty minutes to obtain the benefits of a Noni Eye Poultice.

THE NONI
GARGLE

Noni's analgesic properties can alleviate a sore throat, and its antiseptic properties can fight infection.

TRY THE
NONI GARGLE FOR:

Various throat conditions including:

- Dry throat.
- Sore throat.
- Strep throat.
- Tonsillitis.
- The onset of flu-like symptoms.

267

How to
Gargle with Noni:

1. Take a large sip of Noni fruit juice.

2. Gargle as usual. Allow the juice to gradually drip down your throat.

3. Continue gargling until all the Noni is swallowed.

More about
The Noni Gargle:

Gargle as often as necessary throughout the day.

Gargling with warm Noni Tea (page 115) can also be soothing. But some people may prefer the feeling of gargling with cold Noni, straight from the refrigerator.

You may gargle with some or all of the daily dose of Noni that you would normally drink.

69.

NONI MOUTHWASH

A refreshing and therapeutic alternative to the mint variety.

USE NONI
MOUTHWASH FOR:

- Bad breath.
- Cancer of the mouth.
- Gingivitis.
- Gum and mouth infections.
- Mercury poisoning that affects the gums, tongue, or cheeks.
- Sores on the tongue, gums, or inside the cheeks.
- Toothache.

HOW TO USE
NONI MOUTHWASH:

1. Take a relatively large sip of Noni fruit juice (about one-half a tablespoonful). The juice will cause you to salivate.

2. Swish the Noni-saliva mixture around your teeth and gums and every corner of your mouth. If too much saliva is produced spit out some of the liquid. Continue to swish.

3. After about a minute, the flavor of the Noni will change. This is an indication that your body has absorbed most of the Noni's healing compounds under the tongue. It is also a signal to spit out the Noni-saliva mixture.

MORE ABOUT
NONI MOUTHWASH:

Use the Noni Mouthwash two or three times daily, or as needed.

The swishing movement increases circulation, and allows the Noni to reach the entire mouth. It also incorporates air into the Noni-saliva mixture. The oxygen in this air is one of the reasons the Noni Mouthwash can make your mouth feel so good. The Noni helps carry the oxygen to the cells, oxygenating them. This in turn activates the cells, so they can receive even more of Noni's healing compounds.

You may gargle with Noni Mouthwash. If you do, it is better to gargle first, and then swish the Noni as described above.

A Noni Mouthwash can leave your teeth and gums feeling fresh and clean. It is a wonderful addition to your daily dental care routine.

If you are using the Noni Mouthwash for pain, you may feel relief immediately, or soon afterwards.

A few applications may be necessary to alleviate infection or other acute problems.

Chronic bad breath may require a daily Noni Mouthwash for a long period of time, in addition to drinking Noni every day. Try the Procedure for Chronic Conditions on page 57.

The Noni Mouthwash is not as intense a detoxification as the Oral Detox (page 51). The Noni Mouthwash helps draw toxins from the surface of the mouth, whereas the Oral Detox tends to draw toxins from deeper inside the tissues.

Because the Noni Mouthwash helps draw out toxins from the mouth, try to avoid swallowing it. However, while you are swishing, it is natural to have an urge to swallow. It is possible to allow your body to have this reflex without actually swallowing very much Noni. This is more easily done if you lean forward when the throat muscles contract during the swallow reflex. Don't worry if a little juice drips down your throat.

If you are using the Mouthwash for mercury poisoning, take extra care not to swallow any Noni. Also, the flavor of the Noni may change sooner for you than for most other people, so you may swish for much less than a minute. You should also rinse your mouth with purified water after you spit out the liquid.

70.

NONI
NOSE DROPS

Noni Nose Drops can soothe the sinuses, reduce inflammation, and ease congestion.

USE NONI NOSE DROPS
FOR CONDITIONS SUCH AS:

- Allergies that affect the sinuses.
- Colds and flu.
- Nasal infections.
- Nasal irritations.
- Sinusitis.
- Stuffy nose.

273

HOW TO MAKE
NONI NOSE DROPS:

1. Don't shake the Noni bottle before pouring Noni to make Noni Nose Drops. The watery portion of the juice, found at the top of a new bottle of Noni (which has been left undisturbed), is better for Nose Drops. Too much pulp in the Nose Drops can be mildly irritating.

2. Pour a tablespoonful of Noni fruit juice into a small, clean, glass container. Use a recloseable jar or tincture bottle, or a small glass cup that you can cover with plastic wrap.

3. Measure a tablespoonful of purified water, and pour it into the Noni in a slow, steady, uninterrupted stream. Swirl the liquids together. You have now made Noni Nose Drops.

HOW TO APPLY NONI
NOSE DROPS
METHOD 1:

This may be the easiest of the two methods described in this chapter, but it requires a clean eyedropper.

1. Fill a clean, glass eyedropper with Noni Nose Drops.

2. Hold the eyedropper in a cup of hot tap water to warm the Nose Drops.

3. Squeeze out a drop or two of Nose Drops onto the back of your hand. This serves two purposes: 1) It lets you test the temperature of the liquid. 2) It removes any tap water that might have seeped into the eyedropper while warming it.

4. Tilt your head back, or lie down. Insert a few drops of Noni Nose Drops into each nostril.

SECTION 3 INTERNAL APPLICATIONS

How to Apply Noni
Nose Drops
Method 2:

Use this method if you don't have an eyedropper.

Do not use this method for children because of the small size of their nostrils.

If you would like to warm the Nose Drops, use the heating method for Noni Ear Drops described in the information box on page 255.

1. Shape a piece of cotton ball into a cylinder about one inch long. It should be somewhat less wide than the diameter of your nostril's opening. Taper both ends of the cotton.

2. Saturate one end of the cotton in the Noni Nose Drops solution.

3. Tilt your head back, or lie down. Have a towel or tissue paper handy to catch any Noni Nose Drops that drip on your face.

4. Insert the wet end of the cotton inside your nostril. At least half of the cotton should remain outside your nose.

5. When you insert the cotton, some of the Noni Noni Drops will drip into your nose. To release more liquid from the cotton, gently press the side of your nose against the cotton that is inside it. You will feel the liquid drip into your sinuses.

6. Repeat this procedure for the other nostril, using a second piece of cotton.

More about
Noni Nose Drops:

Noni Nose Drops can be given as often as every few minutes to help clear and soothe the sinuses. Or, apply them a few times a day, as needed.

Remember, Noni is a purplish color and Noni Nose Drops may loosen and dissolve mucus. Don't be surprised when you blow your nose and see purple-stained mucus in the tissue paper.

Store Noni Nose Drops in the refrigerator in a reclosable

glass container. The quantity of Noni Nose Drops solution suggested in the recipe on the previous page will be enough for several applications of Nose Drops. But make a fresh batch each day you plan to use them. At the end of the day, drink any unused Nose Drops that you may have leftover, so they won't be wasted.

THE NONI
RECTAL IMPLANT

Not a place you might expect to put a fruit juice! But if you have problems here, you'll be glad you did.

TRY THE NONI
RECTAL IMPLANT FOR:

Various conditions of the rectum and lower bowel including:

- Cancer.
- Diverticulitis.
- Fissures.
- Hemorrhoids.
- Inflammation.

277

How to do a
Noni Rectal Implant:

1. Purchase a small disposable enema bottle from the drugstore. Open the bottle and pour the prepackaged liquid down the sink. Rinse out the bottle. Pour one or two ounces of Noni fruit juice into the bottle and replace the bottle top.

2. Hold the bottle in a sink full of hot tap water to warm the Noni.

3. Lubricate the bottle tip with an herbal ointment, such as a comfrey or calendula salve. (Don't use petroleum jelly, which will prevent Noni from reaching any area that the petroleum jelly covers. And don't use an ointment that contains menthol—or it will sting.)

4. Find a comfortable position either lying on one side, lying on your back, bending over the sink, or leaning over on your hands and knees. Insert the bottle tip into your rectum. Squeeze the bottle to release the Noni into your body.

5. Hold the Noni in your body for as long as possible. Try to keep it in for at least five minutes. It is best to retain the Noni in your rectum until it is completely absorbed.

More about the
Noni Rectal Implant:

If you have problems of the lower bowel and rectum, it is especially important to apply Noni there directly. When you drink Noni, its healing compounds spread throughout your body. But not enough of these compounds reach the lower bowel and rectum to be therapeutic—though they will help your condition indirectly by uplifting your overall health.

Ideally, try to do the Noni Rectal Implant after you have taken an enema, or have had a bowel movement. Then your rectum will be empty. If you take an enema beforehand, add a tablespoonful of Noni to the enema bag after it has been filled with warm water. It is important to expel as much of the enema into the toilet as possible before doing the Noni Rectal Implant. If too much water remains in your body, you may have a greater-than-usual urge to expel the Implant.

If you have an urge to expel the Implant, try to keep the Implant in for at least a few minutes, then follow the urge. This urge may be your body's way of flushing toxins that the Noni has helped release.

If your body has an immediate strong urge to expel the Implant, use less Noni next time.

If the rectum is highly irritated, the Noni might burn slightly at first. But soothing relief should soon follow.

Perform the Implant daily. If your condition is relatively serious, gradually increase the amount of Noni in the Implant. You can use three to four ounces per treatment. (Disposable enema bottles usually hold up to four ounces of liquid.)

When symptoms subside, gradually reduce the number of times you do the implant each week.

You can reuse the disposable enema bottle if you wash the bottle and the bottle tip with soap and water.

THE SCENT
OF NONI

Not just for those who are sensitive to aromas.

EMPLOY THE SCENT OF NONI TO:

- Focus the effects of Noni on conditions located inside the sinuses, brain, and other organs in the head.

- Enhance the effects of Noni fruit juice, especially when treating conditions that stubbornly resist healing, or that are not responding to Noni fruit juice (or other healing methods), as well as you might expect.

- Invite the vibrations of Noni into your body, in order to provide a pathway for Noni's healing compounds to reach more deeply into more cells.

281

HOW TO EMPLOY
THE SCENT OF NONI:

1. Pour your dose of Noni fruit juice into a cup.

2. Swirl the Noni, as you would a fine wine, to release its aroma.

3. Bring the cup to your face and inhale deeply this aroma several times.

4. Sip the dose. Between sips, again drink in the aroma of Noni fruit juice.

MORE ABOUT
THE SCENT OF NONI:

The raw Noni fruit has an unforgettable smell—in a word, it is nauseating. Fortunately, food scientists have been able to isolate the offending compounds, which have no therapeutic value, and remove them from Noni fruit juice. The juice still has an aroma, but it is not at all unpleasant.

The aroma of something actually consists of molecules of that substance radiating into the air. When you smell the scent of Noni, you are actually breathing in molecules of Noni. In other words, you are drinking in Noni's essence, or vibrations, through your nostrils.

Enjoying the scent of Noni before you drink the juice has advantages. First, it prepares the body to accept Noni's molecules in physical form. Being given fair warning that Noni is coming physically, the body can better decide where to direct Noni's healing compounds. This is true whether you are taking Noni for the first time, or have been drinking Noni for years.

The scent of Noni also introduces Noni to the brain. Making this introduction can be especially helpful when the body is hypersensitive to supplements, or tends to have strong cleansing reactions. After examining Noni's scent, the brain can evaluate whether Noni will be too strong, or introduce changes too quickly. If indeed the brain comes to that conclusion, then the brain will signal the body to be repelled by the Noni's scent, and this will discourage the individual from drinking it. In this case, if you still want to use Noni, it is better to apply Noni topically, or follow the Procedure to Gradually Introduce Noni to the Body (page 81), or follow the Noni Maintenance Dose 4 procedure (page 27). Often the brain will signal the body to reject Noni if the body is dehydrated (page 28, 29). So drinking extra water, in this case, would also be suggested.

If you are a health professional dealing with people who are very sensitive, you can easily discover if Noni will help them—and even to what degree. Simply ask them to sample the scent of Noni as described in the steps on the previous page. If the scent pleases them, it is very likely Noni can help them a great deal. If they find the scent "okay," or "not offensive," then they can benefit from Noni, but maybe not dramatically so.

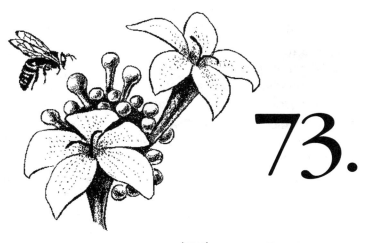

THE NONI
TOOTH AND GUM
COMPRESS

The mouth and gums seem to be more sensitive to Noni's analgesic properties than most other areas of the body.

USE THE NONI TOOTH
AND GUM COMPRESS FOR:

- Gum infection.
- Helping to heal an area after dental work.
- Helping to numb an area before dental work.
- Tooth infection and toothache.

How to Make and Apply
The Noni Tooth and Gum Compress:

1. Make a Tooth and Gum Compress pad using either a cotton ball or sterile gauze. If you use cotton, form it into a cylinder about two inches long and about one-quarter inch wide. If you use gauze, roll it into a cylinder of about the same size.

2. Pour a tablespoonful of Noni fruit juice into a small bowl. Press the compress pad into the Noni. Wipe up any pulp that remains in the bowl with the pulpy side of the compress pad.

3. Insert the wet compress pad into your mouth, with the pulpy side of the pad against your skin. Press the pad above your gum line between the affected area and your cheek. It is okay to swallow any Noni fruit juice that leaks out. However the swallowing action tends to draw the Noni out of the compress. Try to avoid this as much as possible.

4. Leave the compress pad in place for ten to fifteen minutes. By then much of the Noni fruit juice in the pad will have been swallowed and replaced by saliva. Even so, the pulp that clings to the compress pad would still be working.

5. Remove the compress pad and discard it.

6. Repeat the Noni Tooth and Gum Compress as often as needed.

More about the Noni
Tooth and Gum Compress:

Even if the pain is in a small area, make the compress pad about two inches long and treat the entire portion of the jaw where the pain is located. By using a relatively large compress pad, more of Noni's healing compounds will be absorbed into the area. You will then get the most benefit possible from Noni's therapeutic and analgesic properties.

The procedure on the previous page can be used for tooth and gum conditions of all kinds. However, if you have pain from an unfilled tooth cavity, you may benefit by adding to the procedure as follows:

1. Clean out the cavity with a toothbrush.

2. Apply the Noni Tooth and Gum Compress as outlined in Steps 1, 2, and 3 above.

3. Dry the tooth with a clean cloth or piece of gauze.

4. Make a second compress pad using a piece of a cotton ball. It should be small enough to cover the affected tooth. Soak the pad in some Noni fruit juice.

5. Place this second pad over the affected tooth.

6. Press the pad onto the tooth to fill the cavity with Noni. Hold this pad in place with the opposing teeth. Keep both compress pads in place for ten to fifteen minutes. By then, much of the Noni in the pad will have been swallowed or replaced by saliva.

7. Remove both compress pads and discard them. Repeat the above procedure as often as needed.

People have different levels of pain tolerance, so a Tooth and Gum Compress's analgesic effect will vary. Some people may be able to use Noni instead of painkillers during or after routine dental work.

Apply the Noni Tooth and Gum Compress both before and after any dental work you may receive. Doing the Compress beforehand can reduce any traumatic effects you may experience; doing it afterwards can promote healing.

Also try taking a Trauma Dose right before dental work begins, to help you relax and to better handle the stress of dental work.

74.

NONI
TOOTHPASTE

Even your teeth and gums will like Noni.

USE
NONI TOOTHPASTE:

- For daily oral hygiene.
- In addition to using your favorite toothpaste.

How to Use
Noni Toothpaste:

1. Pour about one teaspoonful of Noni fruit juice into a medicine cup and bring it with you to the bathroom.

2. Mentally divide your teeth into four quarters: upper-left, upper-right, lower-left and lower-right.

3. Dip your toothbrush into the Noni. Thoroughly brush the teeth and gums of one quarter of your mouth.

4. Spit out the juice. Rinse your toothbrush and tap out the excess water.

5. Repeat Steps 3 and 4 until you have brushed the teeth in all four quarters of your mouth.

More about
Noni Toothpaste:

Noni Toothpaste leaves your teeth feeling very clean. Since Noni does not contain the fluoride present in conventional toothpaste, it is important to brush with that too. Use Noni Toothpaste in addition to your regular daily dental hygiene program.

In order to use Noni Toothpaste regularly, you will have to find a way to make the technique convenient. In temperate climates you will be able to leave a few teaspoonfuls of Noni on the bathroom counter—enough for a few days—without the Noni spoiling. Otherwise, you could bring some Noni with you to the bathroom each day, although that may soon become bothersome. Or, leave an extra toothbrush nearby the kitchen sink, and brush there daily with Noni.

THE NONI VAGINAL IMPLANT

Noni can be implanted using a small disposable enema bottle, large plastic syringe tube—or even a turkey baster!

USE THE NONI VAGINAL IMPLANT FOR:

Various conditions of the cervix, uterus, and vagina including:

- Cervical Cancer.
- Endometriosis.
- Uterine cancer.
- Uterine prolapse.
- Vaginitis.
- Yeast infections.

How to Apply
The Noni Vaginal Implant:

1. Gather the things you will need to do the implant.

   - A pillow for your head.
   - A rolled up bath towel or another pillow to elevate your hips. (If you use a pillow, cover it with a towel.)
   - A feminine napkin.
   - A panty-liner for afterwards.
   - A small towel for clean up.
   - Something to read to pass the time.

   Use old towels, because Noni fruit juice will stain and getting them wet is unavoidable.

2. Add Noni fruit juice to a plastic syringe tube. This is the best kind of applicator because it allows you to easily control how quickly the Noni is dispensed. The standard dose for a Noni Vaginal Implant is one ounce.

3. Lie on your back, with your hips on the pillow.

4. Put the end of the applicator inside your body and slowly insert the Noni fruit juice. With your other hand, hold the feminine napkin under the syringe, to catch any juice that spills. Try not to cough or sneeze, and try to relax your abdominal muscles. You'll soon discover how best to relax in order to retain as much of the Noni as possible.

5. After you have inserted the Noni, remain lying in this position for about 15 to 20 minutes.

6. When you are ready to get up, hold the feminine napkin and the small towel between your legs to catch the juice. Most of it will spill out when you rise.

7. Wear the panty-liner to collect any remaining Noni that may leak out later.

MORE ABOUT THE
NONI VAGINAL IMPLANT:

The Noni Vaginal Implant is usually performed once a day. However, consider doing the Implant twice a day if it results in foul odor, mucus discharge, or tissue sloughing. This indicates the Implant is causing significant cleansing and should be done more than once a day to support the vaginal detoxification.

Plastic syringe tubes are the easiest applicators to use. They can be purchased at pet stores, especially those that specialize in large birds. (They are intended for hand-feeding large baby parrots.)

Find a syringe that holds two ounces of liquid. The plunger in a one-ounce syringe tends to fall out easily when the syringe contains a full ounce of liquid. If you use a one-ounce syringe because that's all you can find, fill it twice using half an ounce of liquid each time.

You may not need to warm the juice as you would for Noni Ear Drops or Eye Drops, because the vaginal tissue is less sensitive to temperature.

It may be more convenient to do the Vaginal Implant when you are in bed for the night. Then you can keep the Noni inside your body longer—at least until you get out of bed. Just keep your bed linens well protected, and have old towels ready to catch the juice when you do get up.

If you have a prolapse, it will be difficult to implant much juice at first. Start with one-half ounce of Noni and work up to an ounce as the condition improves. Even if you use only one-half ounce of Noni, you may be able to insert only a small portion of this at a time. Hold as much of it inside you as you can; though it may leak right out, just insert a little more. Do this until the entire half ounce of Noni has been used.

Though the Noni used in the Vaginal Implant won't come into direct contact with the ovaries, the Vaginal Implant can still be helpful for ovarian conditions. The Vaginal Implant will help uplift the health of the entire female reproductive system, which includes the ovaries, and may provide a pathway for toxins in the ovaries to leave the body.

Because the Implant uplifts the health of the entire area, the Implant can also be helpful for endometriosis. For this condition, also apply a Noni Poultice (page 147), Noni Paste (page 153), or Noni–clay (page 159), over the areas of pain.

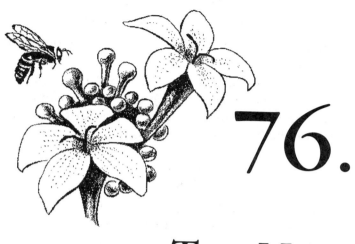

THE NONI
VAGINAL WIPE

A fast and easy way to alleviate minor discomforts.

WHEN TO USE
THE NONI VAGINAL WIPE:

- After childbirth.
- For vaginal itching.
- For mild yeast infections.
- To freshen up after intercourse.
- To soothe chapped, irritated, or dry labia.

HOW TO APPLY
THE NONI VAGINAL WIPE:

1. Dip a cotton ball in Noni fruit juice, so that only half of it gets wet.

2. Wipe the wet side of the cotton ball inside the vaginal opening. Then wipe between the labia. Squeeze the cotton ball as you apply it, or press it against your body, to release the Noni onto your skin.

MORE ABOUT THE
NONI VAGINAL WIPE:

This procedure can be done after every urination, or as needed.

Press the wet cotton against particularly sore or itchy areas to release the juice directly onto those areas.

Relief may come on contact with the Noni, or several minutes later. Several applications may be needed. For more serious conditions, apply a Noni Compress (page 143) over the area or try a Noni Vaginal Implant (page 291). You can also insert the Noni–soaked cotton ball that you used in Steps 1 and 2 into your vagina. Replace it several times a day with another cotton ball soaked with Noni.

After childbirth, your labia may be too tender to apply Noni with a cotton ball. Instead, add a tablespoonful or more of Noni to a sani-bottle that has been filled with warm water. After urination, squirt the Noni-water mixture onto your labia. This can feel especially soothing.

APPENDIX A

HEALTH
EVALUATION SHEETS

Healing is a natural function of the body. It is also natural to forget we ever had certain symptoms once they've gone away. This questionnaire will help you remember the symptoms you used to have, so you can better appreciate the difference in how you feel now.

USE THESE HEALTH
EVALUATION SHEETS FOR:

- Keeping track of your health progress.
- Evaluating how well Noni has helped you.
- Evaluating the effectiveness of certain Noni dosages and applications.

(cont.)

- Your personal testimony to the effects of Noni, which you can keep confidential, or share with your doctor, or your family, friends, and associates.

HOW TO USE THESE
HEALTH EVALUATION SHEETS:

1. Complete Part 1 before you start taking Noni fruit juice (or as soon as possible thereafter). Give brief, honest answers. When you have finished Part 1, don't look at what you've written until after you have completed Part 2.

2. Make some copies of Part 2.*

3. After taking Noni daily for about a month or two, complete a copy of Part 2.

4. Compare your answers on Part 2, with what you wrote earlier on Part 1. Use a marking pen to highlight those answers that are significantly different.

5. A few months later, complete another copy of Part 2. Compare your answers with those you gave on evaluation sheets you had previously completed. Use what you learn from these evaluation sheets to adjust how you are using Noni.

6. From time to time, monitor your health progress by completing another copy of Part 2.

HEALTH EVALUATION SHEET - PART 1

Please complete the following sentences before you start to take Noni, or as soon as possible there-after:

Overall, my health is _____

Five parts of my body that I consider unhealthy are: 1) _____
2) _____ 3) _____ 4) _____ 5) _____

These areas have bothered me for how long?: 1) _____ 2) _____ 3) _____ 4) _____ 5) _____
(Numbers here correspond to numbers above.)

I would describe my worst pain as _____

When I wake up in the morning, my pain is _____

When it's bedtime, my pain is _____

After I eat, my body feels _____

My bowel and bladder regularity is _____

My menstrual cycles are _____

300

My libido is _____

My skin feels _____

My hands feel _____

My feet feel _____

My joints feel _____

My circulation is _____

My body weight seems _____

In general, my emotions are _____

My mental clarity and memory is _____

I am taking Noni fruit juice for _____

I think Noni fruit juice will _____

The one thing I would like most to change about my health is _____

HEALTH EVALUATION SHEET - PART 2

Please complete the following sentences after you have taken Noni for a while:

Overall, my health is _____

Five parts of my body that I consider unhealthy are: 1) _____ 5) _____
2) _____ 3) _____ 4) _____

These areas have bothered me for how long?: 1) _____ 2) _____ 3) _____ 4) _____ 5) _____
(Numbers here correspond to numbers above.)

I would describe my worst pain as _____

When I wake up in the morning, my pain is _____

When it's bedtime, my pain is _____

After I eat, my body feels _____

My bowel and bladder regularity is _____

My menstrual cycles are _____

My libido is _____

My skin feels _____

My hands feel _____

My feet feel _____

My joints feel _____

My circulation is _____

My body weight seems _____

In general, my emotions are _____

My mental clarity and memory is _____

I am taking Noni fruit juice for _____

I think Noni fruit juice will _____

The one thing I would like most to change about my health is ____

APPENDIX B

CLEANSING
REACTIONS

The body naturally cleanses itself of toxins and metabolic wastes all the time. A cleansing reaction (also called a healing crisis or detoxification crisis) may occur when something that promotes good health, like Noni fruit juice, helps your body release more toxins than your organs can handle at once.

COMMON CLEANSING
REACTIONS INCLUDE:

- Bad breath or body odor.
- Boils and pimples.
- Cough.
- Diarrhea or loose stools.
  (cont.)

- Emotional releases.

- Foul smelling urine.

- Headaches.

- Heavier than usual bleeding at menstruation.

- Intestinal gas or bloating.

- Joint pain due to release of uric acid crystals.

- Mucus discharge.

- Skin rashes.

- Swollen glands.

- Unusual fatigue.

HOW DO I KNOW IF I'M HAVING A CLEANSING REACTION?

Sometimes it can be difficult to know the difference between a cleansing reaction, an allergic reaction, or hyper-sensitivity to Noni's healing compounds.

The symptoms listed above may also indicate disease or illness, especially if they are long-standing. This chapter focuses on symptoms which occur suddenly, and which can be linked to taking Noni fruit juice.

If you get a reaction <u>immediately</u> after taking Noni:

- You may have an allergy to Noni.

  Suspect that this is the case if your symptoms include your body's typical responses to things you are allergic to. Wait until your symptoms subside. Then try a Noni Tummy Treatment (page 237 and 243). The skin may be an effective barrier to your allergic reaction, while also allowing you to receive the benefits of Noni's healing compounds.

  If the Tummy Treatment gives you a rash, or you get another sign of an allergy, you probably are allergic to Noni. It may be best not to take Noni at this time.

- You might be hypersensitive to Noni's healing compounds.

  Suspect that this is the case if your symptoms do not include your body's typical responses to things you are allergic to. Wait until your symptoms subside. Then try a Noni Tummy Treatment (page 237 and 243). The Tummy Treatment can help your body adjust gradually to Noni. If you do not get a rash or any other cleansing reaction, continue the topical application daily. Give your body time to become accustomed to Noni. Use the Procedure to Gradually Introduce Noni to the Body (page 81).

- You may be having an immediate cleansing reaction.

  Suspect that this is the case if:

  - Your symptoms include foul odors, and are unlike your body's typical responses to things you are allergic to.

  - Your body was already primed for a cleansing, and Noni just provided the supportive boost needed to proceed.

  - You have been drinking less than two glasses of water a day and toxins have been building up in your body.

    Make sure you are drinking at least eight glasses of purified water a day, to flush the metabolic wastes your body naturally produces, plus the toxins your body collects from your diet and from the environment. If you have not been drinking enough water and you get a cleansing reaction, your symptoms can go away if you simply drink more water.

  The following day, try another dose of Noni. If the Noni eases your symptoms, you have likely had an immediate cleansing reaction. Continue to take Noni to assist your body through the cleanse.

  See pages 28 and 29 to read about symptoms that can appear like a cleansing, but are really caused by drinking Noni when the body is dehydrated.

If you have been taking Noni for a while, and then get cleansing symptoms:

- You are probably not allergic to Noni or hypersensitive to Noni's healing compounds, since you have been taking Noni for a while without having had a reaction.

- You may be experiencing either a cleansing reaction or the flu. It can be hard to know which is which because:

  - Both cleansing reactions and the flu tend to last the same amount of time. Both can be acute and short-lived; however, both can also drag out for quite a while.

  - Natural methods for enhancing the immune system will help in either case.

  - Antibiotics, cough-suppressants, and other pharmaceutical medicines often suppress a cleansing reaction. But they may be necessary in some cases to stabilize the body, so it can gain strength for a more gradual detoxification later.

> Please see a Health Professional if your symptoms become more than you can comfortably address with home remedies.

You probably have a cold or flu if:

You have been taking a Maintenance Dose of one ounce daily. Generally, one ounce a day of Noni is enough to supply the body's daily need for Noni's healing compounds. It is unlikely that this much Noni would initiate a cleansing reaction in most people.

You are probably having a cleansing reaction if you are doing or have recently done:

- The Top Dose Procedure.
- A Noni Fast.
- The Technique for Stubborn Conditions.

WHAT TO DO IF YOU THINK
YOU ARE HAVING A CLEANSING REACTION:

Here are some ways you can use Noni to ease your cleansing symptoms if you think you may be having a cleansing reaction:

- Make sure you drink at least eight glasses of purified water a day. Water is essential to help flush toxins out of the system.

- Substitute a dose of Noni Tea (page 115) for each dose of Noni that you usually take.

- Drink an extra dose or two of Noni, in the form of Noni Tea.

- Try taking the same number of doses as usual, but take only about half a tablespoonful each time as an Auto-dilution (page 47).

- Use the Noni Tummy Treatment either in place of your regular Noni doses, or in addition to them.

- Try drinking a half a glass of water both before and after taking a dose of Noni. This will encourage Noni's healing compounds to enter your body more gradually—with less immediate impact. Those who feel their body is particularly toxic may try this technique with every dose of Noni that they take, in order to encourage a more gradual detoxification. (See maintenance Dose 4, pages 27-30.)

- Try the Noni Fast Method 2 (page 107).

- Combine Noni fruit juice with other modalities. Noni is compatible with all natural healing methods including: herbs, homeopathic remedies, chiropractic, Chinese Medicine, Ayurvedic Medicine, Bach flower essences, vitamins and minerals, chelation therapy, acupuncture, massage, and others.

> In general, any reaction to Noni is better than no reaction at all. The reaction proves that your body recognizes Noni and that Noni can indeed affect you. Now the goal is to figure out what amounts, dosages, and applications of Noni your body needs to function at its best.

Positive
Cleansing Reactions:

Although cleansing reactions have a reputation for being associated with unpleasant symptoms, they can also be positive. Unfortunately, positive cleansing reactions don't last as long as we might like them to. Positive reactions include:

- Greatly improved memory.
- Remarkably clearer thinking.
- A surge of creativity and new ideas.
- An extraordinary sense of well being.
- Considerably more energy than usual.
- An unusual clarity and insight into the meaning of one's life.
- Dreams which are easier to remember, more profound, and more meaningful.
- A profound ability to see the overview of life itself, or of various situations that we may be involved with.
- Unusual hypersensitivity to one's own thoughts, needs and feelings, as well as to those of others.

Naturally, we welcome the positive cleansing reactions, but try not to be disappointed when they go away. Your body will soon adjust to the greater level of health, and the positive reactions will lessen as you settle into a new, healthier state of "normal." Continue to take Noni to help maintain this higher level of health.

More about
Cleansing Reactions

Old injuries and health challenges, and particularly intense emotions may also surface briefly. This also indicates a kind of cleansing reaction. Old injuries and conditions tend to arise in reverse order, as progressively older conditions are re-experienced. They will soon pass if their healing process is given adequate support. Be sure to address them with the appropriate topical and internal Noni applications, in addition to your daily oral doses of Noni.

Loose stools tend to occur when you are taking more Noni than you need. This may occur, for example, if you are a nursing mother taking extra Noni for a sick baby. The Noni you drink will pass into your breastmilk. You will have to weigh the benefits of the Noni for your baby against the relative inconvenience of frequent visits to the bathroom.

Ideally, using Noni should allow you to detoxify gradually and feel good at the same time. Then, if you do have a cleansing reaction, adjusting the amount of Noni you take and how you take it can help you detoxify more comfortably.

APPENDIX C

WHAT IF NONI DOESN'T SEEM TO WORK FOR ME?

If Noni doesn't seem to be helping or isn't working as fast as you would like, ask yourself the following questions. The answers may help you understand what may be happening, and give you some ideas about what to do.

FOR WHAT CONDITION ARE YOU TAKING NONI?

It helps to decide why you are taking Noni. This makes it easier to correlate Noni's effects with changes in your health.

HOW LONG HAVE YOU HAD THIS CONDITION?

If your condition is chronic and long-standing, you may need more time on any health improvement program before you see results. In the process of healing, healthier cells replace sick or damaged cells. This always seems to take longer than one would like. You probably won't feel a difference in your health until enough of these replacements have been made.

How long have you been taking Noni?

In some cases, it can take several months before you enjoy positive changes in your health. Give Noni a fair chance to work, and give yourself a fair opportunity to heal.

How much Noni fruit juice are you taking?

Some people's bodies need more Noni than others do, even for maintenance. In general, the more serious the condition the more Noni you may need.

Are you taking Noni fruit juice regularly?

When addressing any health condition with Noni fruit juice, it is important to take your doses regularly. Make sure you have enough juice on hand so you won't run out.

Have you filled out Part 1 of the Health Evaluation Sheets, in Appendix A?

If you have, maybe now is the time to fill out the second sheet (Part 2) and compare your health then and now.

If you have not filled out the sheet, try to remember what your condition was like before you started to take Noni. Write down what symptoms you had. How severe were they? Take an honest look at how you feel now. Is there any difference at all?

Ask a friend or family member to recall your state of health and well being before you began taking Noni, and to evaluate your health as it is now. This feedback will be invaluable. In fact, it can be more helpful than your own evaluation, in deciding how well Noni is working for you.

HAVE YOU NOTICED ANY UNEXPECTED CHANGES IN YOUR HEALTH?

Have you noticed any improvement in minor discomforts? It is easy to overlook these kinds of improvements, especially if you are taking Noni for a major health challenge. (For example, I had no idea my eyesight had improved until someone mentioned that theirs had. I may never have noticed otherwise. I also thought that having a small amount of vaginal discharge daily was normal—until it went away after taking Noni!)

HAVE YOU HAD ANY CLEANSING REACTIONS SINCE YOU STARTED TAKING NONI?

For a list of common cleansing reactions, see pages 305-306. Cleansing reactions, though generally uncomfortable, should be considered beneficial because they signal that the body is experiencing a major cleansing. Detoxification is often a necessary first step before cell repair and health building can begin.

DID NONI EVER WORK FOR YOU AT ALL?

There is a difference between the experience of not ever having noticed any effects from Noni at all, either positive or negative, and the experience of noticing a difference at first, and then nothing thereafter.

If you have never, ever noticed anything from Noni, and you have been taking Noni for at least a few months, then perhaps your body simply doesn't need Noni's healing compounds. Or maybe your body doesn't know how to put these compounds to good use.

If you noticed a difference at first, and then nothing since, you know that Noni can help you. It may now be working below the threshold of your ability to perceive its effects. Or, it may be helping you to maintain your present level of health, and preventing it from getting worse.

Try increasing your daily dose of Noni. You might also try the Top Dose Procedure (page 35), the Technique for Stubborn Conditions (page 77), or one of the Noni Fasts (pages 103, 107, or 111).

What about positive changes in your personality, emotions, mental clarity, or memory?

Sometimes Noni seems to work on our non-physical aspects first. We may become more patient, calm, joyful, better able to handle stress and emotions, or perhaps less irritable, impatient, or moody. Don't overlook these possible health benefits as well.

Are you taking other health supplements?

Noni is not a cure-all. Although Noni provides important micronutrients, it does not supply all the micronutrients that the body needs. It is possible that your condition would benefit from other supplements. Try a full-spectrum vitamin and mineral supplement, which would help meet all your nutrient requirements.

What activities do you now enjoy since you began to take Noni?

Sometimes the best gauge of improved health is not how we feel, but how well we can enjoy life.

APPENDIX D

WHAT IF MY
SYMPTOMS RETURN?

Some people find that after Noni alleviates certain symptoms, these symptoms eventually return. It is tempting to say that Noni has stopped working. But this is not necessarily the case. Here are a few possible explanations, plus some ideas for how you can use Noni if your symptoms do come back.

- Many people who start taking Noni say they feel better almost right away. They may be experiencing positive cleansing reactions (page 310), which may be making them feel so good, they don't notice their symptoms. Unfortunately, their symptoms will probably "return" when the positive cleansing reactions no longer mask them. Lasting positive changes in one's health won't occur until they are supported by actual changes in the cells. These changes usually take time.

- After taking Noni, many people find they can eat foods that once before caused certain symptoms such as indigestion, headaches, or joint pain. They find they can work harder, play harder, go to bed later and get up earlier, too.

  Instead of using Noni's healing compounds to help us grow healthier, we often use them to help us get away with doing things that are stressful (albeit enjoyable). There is nothing wrong with this. But if we abuse the freedom, it won't last.

  When the body can no longer handle the added stress, we will again need more sleep, and favorite foods will again cause discomfort. Symptoms may appear to return, when really they weren't given the opportunity to heal in the first place.

- The body will continue to age and manifest stress at its weakest points, no matter how wonderful the therapies are that we give to it. If new stresses are introduced into our lives, these weakest points may again reveal themselves and conditions that were once alleviated may return.

- During the healing process, pain and other symptoms may go away. But this doesn't mean our ailment is cured. It can take a while for healthy cells to replace unhealthy cells. Meanwhile, we may become more active than before, and cause additional stress on the healing tissue. Symptoms may return, simply to remind us to take better care of ourselves.

- Health improves in cycles: A period of health building follows every period of well being. This health-building period may pass unnoticed or make us feel more tired than usual. Or it may include an intense cleansing, when the body releases toxins, wastes, fat, and various excesses that it may have been storing. As these toxins enter the bloodstream, they pass by our weak or problem areas. These toxins can irritate these areas, causing symptoms to temporarily resurface or get worse.

- Symptoms can be signals to take better care of ourselves. Recurring symptoms may be our body's best way to tell us we need something that we have not yet given to our body. Perhaps we need more rest, or a nutrient that is missing from our diet.

- Recurring symptoms may also alert us to look at our condition from another angle. Perhaps there are mental or emotional causes that we have been overlooking. Sometimes physical improvement cannot continue until we take care of the mental and emotional aspects of ourselves.

- Dr. Ralph Heinicke offered yet another explanation for why symptoms may return, in a letter he wrote to me in October, 1997. He writes, "I now believe that some people have a marginal supply of several crucial micronutrients. Initially proxeronine is the limiting factor. This explains the tremendous response [from taking Noni], which some people observe. However, after taking Noni for a while, other micronutrients become limiting factors for good health."

  Dr. Heinicke then offers two approaches, "1) to discover what the next specific health limiting factor is, or 2) to take a supplement which contains a wide variety of potentially limiting factors."

Returning symptoms often go away again after Interrupting Noni Therapy (page 39) for a few days. In fact, after resuming Noni, health sometimes takes a leap for the better.

Here are some ideas that may explain why Interrupting Noni Therapy works:

- Symptoms may return if the body becomes accustomed to Noni's healing compounds. To obtain the same results as before, the body would need greater amounts of Noni. Taking larger doses may indeed help—for a while.

Interrupting Noni Therapy seems to readjust the body's relationship to Noni's healing compounds. Then, the smaller, and/or previous dosages of Noni become helpful once again.

- The cells in our body are innately intelligent, and like us, they have a memory and can take on both good and bad habits. As new cells replace old cells, the new cells may not remember how conditions once were without Noni. They may take the now-constant supply of Noni's healing compounds for granted and not use them as best as they could. Interrupting Noni Therapy encourages the cells to use these compounds more effectively and efficiently.

- Another possibility is that when certain unused Noni compounds are stored in the body for too long, they may start to cause stress. Perhaps they deteriorate into other compounds. If this is so, maybe Interrupting Noni Therapy clears out the old stores. Then Noni usually works just as well, if not better, than it did before.

If your symptoms return, but it is not appropriate to Interrupt Noni Therapy because you have immune deficiency conditions, diabetes, cancer, or a life-threatening condition, here are some techniques you could try:

- Take sips of your doses on a regular time schedule. For example, take a sip every five, fifteen, or sixty minutes. Set a timer to ensure you keep to the rhythm.

- Try the Auto-dilution (page 47) and the Noni Tummy Treatment (pages 237 and 243). Also try other topical and internal Noni applications that are appropriate for your condition.

- Try Sipping (page 43) your doses of Noni if you usually drink them All-at-Once (page 45). Or, try drinking them All-at-Once if you usually Sip them.

- Examine your diet and lifestyle. Are you taking part in any activities that might be stressing your body? Find out what foods you may be allergic to, and eliminate them from your diet. Some Health Practitioners have ways to test for allergies, which can give you immediate feedback. Get more rest, try meditation or spiritual exercise, and take better care of yourself emotionally, mentally, physically, and spiritually.

ENDNOTES

[1] Neil Solomon, M.D. Ph.D., *Tahitian Noni Juice: How Much How Often for What* (Vineyard: Direct Source Publishing, 2000), pp. 2, 3.

[2] *Noni—Polynesia's Natural Pharmacy* (Vineyard: Pride Publishing, 1997), pp. 17, 18.

[3] Julia Morton, "The Ocean-Going Noni, or Indian Mulberry and Some of Its Colorful Relatives," *Economic Botany*, Vol. 46 (3), 1992.

[4] Chafique Younos, Alain Rolland, Jacques Fleurentin, Marie-Claire Lanhers, Rene Misslin, and Francois Mortier, "Analgesic and Behavioral Effects of *Morinda citrifolia*," *Planta Med*, Vol. 56, 1990.

[5] Tomonori Hiramatsu, Masaya Imoto, Takashi Koyano, Kazuo Umezawa, "Induction of Normal Phenotypes in *Ras*-Transformed Cells by Damnacanthal from *Morinda citrifolia*," *Cancer Letters*, Vol. 73, 1993.

[6] R. M. Heinicke, "The Pharmacologically Active Ingredient of Noni," University of Hawaii. (Http://www.hookele.com /noni/active.html).

[7] Fleur L. Strand, *Physiology: A Regulatory Systems Approach*, (New York: Macmillan, 1978), pp. 31, 56, 57, 63.

8 R. M. Heinicke, "The Pharmacologically Active Ingredient of Noni," (Http://www.hookele.com/Noni/active.html).

9 Neil Solomon, M.D. Ph.D., *Tahitian Noni Juice: How Much How Often for What* (Vineyard: Direct Source Publishing, 2000).

10 *Noni—Polynesia's Natural Pharmacy* (Vineyard: Pride Publishing, 1997), 500 South Geneva Road, Vineyard, UT, 84058. 1-800-748-2996.

11 Rita Elkins M.H., "Noni *(Morinda citrifolia)* Prize Herb of the South Pacific" (Pleasant Grove: Woodland Publishing, 1997), P.O. Box 160, Pleasant Grove, UT 84062.

12 Neil Solomon, M.D. Ph.D., *Part of the Tahitian Noni Smart Extracts Series: Original Extract* (Vineyard: Direct Source Publishing, 2000), pp. 16, 17.

13 Notes taken during a Question and Answer period featuring Dr. Ralph Heinicke, at the 1997 Morinda™, Inc. Conference, August 12, 1997, Las Vegas, Nevada.

14 Dr. Ralph Heinicke, *"Cell Regeneration: Unlocking the Secrets of Tahitian Noni."* audiocassette, copyright ©1996 Morinda™, Inc.

15 http://www.healthy.net/asp/templates/article.asp?id=1278

16 Notes taken during a Question and Answer period featuring Dr. Ralph Heinicke, at the 1997 Morinda™, Inc. Conference, August 12, 1997, Las Vegas, Nevada.

17 *American Red Cross: Community First Aid & Safety* (St Louis: Mosby Lifeline, 1993), p. 147.

18 *Understanding the Miracle: An Introduction to the Science of Noni,* A series of interviews conducted by A.K. Olsen with Dr. Ralph Heinicke, from June 1998 to August 1998 (Direct Source, 1-800-748-2996), p. 14.

19 Raymond Dextreit and Michel Abehsera, *Our Earth Our*

Cure (New York: Swan House Publishing, 1979), p. 17.

[20] ibid. p. 22.

[21] ibid. p. 20.

[22] *American Red Cross: Community First Aid & Safety* (St Louis: Mosby Lifeline, 1993), p. 147.

[23] ibid.

[24] ibid.

[25] ibid.

[26] ibid.

[27] *Reader's Digest Action Guide: What to do in an Emergency,* pp. 7-9

[28] *American Red Cross: Community First Aid & Safety,* p. 147.

[29] Dr. Ralph Heinicke, *"Cell Regeneration: Unlocking the Secrets of Tahitian Noni,"* audiocassette, copyright © 1996, Morinda™, Inc.

INDEX

O

Note from the Author

Dear Reader,

I hope you enjoyed *76 Ways to Use Noni* and that you found it helpful. Noni fruit is such an amazing all-natural pharmacopoeia. It truly is a privilege to be able to write about it and share what I have learned with Noni enthusiasts around the world.

I would love to hear from you, and invite you to write me in care of the publisher, who has agreed to forward my mail. Please write: Isa Navarre, c/o Pride Publishing, 15 East 400 South, Orem Utah, U.S.A. 84058.

You are also welcome to visit my website: www.isanavarre.com. I offer information about each of my Noni books as well as a gallery of my fiber art landscapes for you to enjoy. Visit periodically for news and announcements about my upcoming books, plus new information about Noni that I will be posting from time to time.

Thank you for all your support, and have a wonderful life!

Sincerely,

–Isa